Understanding
Biblical Kingdoms & Empires

An Introductory Atlas
& Comparative View

PAUL H. WRIGHT

cartaJerusalem

Contents

List of Maps

Copyright © 2010
Carta Jerusalem, Ltd.
18 Ha'uman Street, P.O.B. 2500, Jerusalem 9102401, Israel
www.carta-jerusalem.com
E-mail: carta@carta.co.il

Cartography: Carta, Jerusalem

Photographs: Paul H. Wright

ISBN: 978-965-220-786-9

Printed in Israel

On the Edge of Empire in a Land Between[1]

Though centered in the southern Levant, the world of the Bible is much larger, stretching across the ancient Near East and filling the brim of the eastern Mediterranean Basin. The former traces the arc of the Fertile Crescent from the Persian Gulf up the broad river valleys of the Tigris and Euphrates, then downward to the Nile. The latter takes in the sweep of lands bordering the Great Sea (so it was called by the biblical writers; cf. Josh 15:12; 23:4; Ezek 47:10) from the boot of Italy through the Aegean and Anatolia to Egypt, then westward along the north African coast to Carthage (modern Tunisia). The Levant, the eastern seaboard of the Mediterranean, is the seam that binds these two great arenas together, and as the homeland core of the biblical story it looked, for better or worse, both ways.

None of the great empires of the ancient Near East or the Mediterranean Basin were born in the Levant. The powers that became Egypt, the Hittites, Assyria, Babylon, Persia, Greece and Rome all began elsewhere, in lands blessed with resource bases that were more than adequate to prompt urbanization, fuel expansion and, eventually, burst into the full bloom of Empire. Moreover, none were ever really at home in the Levant, either. Rather, they arrived in a succession of waves, inundated the coast and broad inland valleys that cradled the imperial highways of the ancient world, then flowed on. Sometimes the flood reached high into the hills:

> Now therefore, behold, the LORD is about to bring on [Judah]
>> the strong and abundant water of the Euphrates,
>>> the king of Assyria and all his glory;
>> and it will rise up over all its channels and go over all its banks.
> Then it will sweep on into Judah,
>> it will overflow and pass through,
>>> it will reach even to the neck,

and the spread of its wings will fill the breadth of your land,
O Immanuel (Isa 8:7–8)

This image, while odd for the dry highland hills of Judah, fit the broad river valleys of the Euphrates and Nile exactly (cf. Jer 46:8; Amos 8:8; 9:5) where, like clockwork, floodwaters brought yearly doses of life (a renewed covering of silt) and death (inundated homes and unchecked disease) to the lands they touched. For the shepherds and villagers of the southern Levant the armies of the ancient world never seemed to stop flowing through, and while an opportunistic few who lived on the highway seized the moment to bask in the influx of new ideas and economic opportunities that invariably came their way as the initial penetration subsided, the majority saw only destruction in its wake.

With a few notable exceptions (e.g. timber from Lebanon or salt and bitumen from the Dead Sea), the great empires of the ancient world did not want the Levant because of its resources *per se*, but because the eastern seaboard of the Mediterranean offered the best (and in some cases, only) land route to the revenue priorities of the closest empire beyond. It wasn't for lack of grain in Egypt that Thutmose III raided the wheat fields of the Jezreel Valley after his bold conquest of Megiddo in the mid-fifteenth century B.C., but to feed the belly of his still-advancing army and simply claim the victor's spoils.[2] (Unlike the image of a flood, Joel's vision of a grain-devouring locust invasion *was* a reality that Judah feared; Joel 1:4–7.) Assyria wanted the resources of Anatolia and Egypt; Babylon drove through Assyria before it headed toward Egypt; Persia was after Anatolia and Greece, but also had its eyes on the revenue of Egypt. Rome had to first secure the eastern bend of the Mediterranean in order to ensure that the wealth of Egypt, of the Arabian Peninsula and, hopefully, that of the Euphrates Valley, flowed west.

PHYSICAL MAP OF THE ANCIENT NEAR EAST

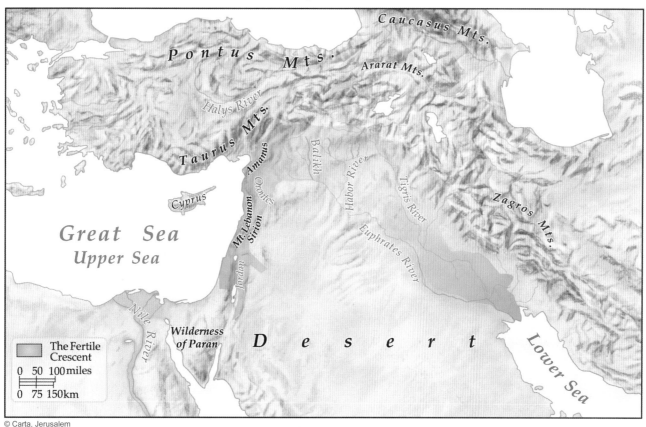

The Fertile Crescent

0 50 100 miles

0 75 150 km

The ever-green fields of Egypt cast a powerful spell over all of the empires of the ancient Near East, and provided a source of wealth that bent all roads to the Nile.

For its part, Egypt—the land coveted by all—cast its eyes in turn on the sources of wealth controlled by everyone else. The Levant, the Land Between (in the words of James Monson[3]), was exactly that—a land bridge to cross on the hunt for larger prizes further afield, but also a conduit of flowing revenue to divert on the way. While exceptions can be found, the overall pattern in the historical record of the peoples of the ancient Near East and Mediterranean Basin portrays the Levant as a frontier of Empire: a bridge to cross, and a buffer to hold.

In contrast, for the smaller nation-states who made the Levant their home, the hills and valleys lining the eastern seaboard of the Mediterranean offered first and foremost a place to settle down and stay. Some, such as Philistia, Ammon, Moab, Edom and the Arameans of Damascus (Syria)—all names familiar to readers of the Hebrew Bible—sat astride the same longitudinal land routes that connected the great empires circling the horizon like vultures. Phoenicia, similarly, held the most favored terminus of the Mediterranean's eastern sea routes. The Northern Kingdom of Israel straddled the imperial highway whenever it was able to control the crossroads that was the Jezreel Valley. Judah alone was essentially off-route, comfortable enough in the hills rising from the coast and only occasionally able to penetrate lowland zones along its edges that were otherwise defined as being international. All had chances, for better or worse, to tap into the imperial routes of the Levant—and face the consequences of Empire in the process. And through it all, it was Judah—the Judeans or Jews—who proved most adept at the role of survivor, and it is their story, immortalized in the records of the Bible, that carried the day.

When mapping the homeland of Empire a place is often reserved for David and Solomon who, from Jerusalem, were able to control the entire Levant "from the River [Euphrates] to the land of the Philistines and to the border of Egypt" (1 Kgs 4:21; cf. Gen 15:18–21). Moreover, these first kings of Israel put an administrative framework in place that was reminiscent of that of the marvelously efficient New Kingdom of Egypt. But though certainly impressive by local standards, Solomon's empire never encompassed an area that rivaled in size that of the great empires of the ancient world, or ever conquered any of those empires' heartlands (even though all were weak or non-existent at the time). Perhaps more tellingly, Solomon's empire failed to last beyond a single generation, its future ripped to shreds by Shishak of Egypt five years after Solomon's death (1 Kgs 14:25–28; 2 Chronicles 12:1–12).[4] Nevertheless, the efforts of David and Solomon to create and maintain an empire are exceptional, and this, along with the vision of the most successful of their heirs—kings such as Ahab, Jehoshaphat, Hezekiah, Josiah and the Hasmonean dynasty half a millennium later—serves as a kind of template by which the political successes of ancient Israel can be measured. So, to, the messages of the Bible's great prophets, whose voices rang most clear when their nation was under direct threat from empires without and injustices within.

The story of ancient Israel, then, can be read two ways: from the vantage point of the great empires of the ancient Near East and Mediterranean Basin who sought to impose their will on the land that lay between, but also through the eyes of the kings and prophets of ancient Israel and Judah who, by the sheer force of geography, were never uninterested bystanders. A comparative view allows the student of the ancient world to look both ways in the never ending attempt to understand oneself, and the other.

A bedouin tent amidst the ruins of the once and still grand city of Jerash reflects the timelessness of carved stone and goat-hair cloth—Empire and commoner—in the ancient lands of the Bible.

The Old Babylonian Empire and the Origin of the People of Israel

The Bible regards Moses as the founder of the nation and religion of ancient Israel, but traces Israel's history and an awareness of God's call on human life all the way back to Abraham (Gen 12:1–9; 15:1–21). The narratives of the lives of the patriarchs recorded in the biblical book of Genesis, together with reflections in subsequent books of the Hebrew Bible and New Testament, offer an intimate account of ancient Israel's earliest origins. The Bible's own internal chronology, read with all due attention to the kind of patterning that characterizes genealogical material of the ancient world, suggests a date for the patriarchs somewhere in the Middle Bronze Age II (c. 2000–1550 B.C.; cf. Gen 15:13, 16; Ex 12:40–41; 1 Kgs 6:1). This period, which was dominated in Mesopotamia by the Old Babylonian Empire (also called the First Dynasty of Babylon; 1894–1595[5]), offers a comfortable cultural context by which to read the patriarchal accounts.

The start of the second millennium B.C. saw the rise of an emerging world awareness that had been present only in incipient form in the centuries prior. Land that in the third millennium B.C. had been under the political and economic control of a confederation of Sumerian city-states centered in lower Mesopotamia (Ur III) came under the sway of a Semitic people (or peoples) of Amorite (Amurrite) origins. Although we don't have a single text written in Amorite, the presence of the Amorites is nonetheless known to have been felt all across the ancient Near East in the first half of the second millennium B.C. The name Amorite (MAR.TU in Sumerian and *Amurru* in Akkadian), which means "Westerner," speaks of both ethnicity and homeland, and places Amorite origins in Upper Mesopotamia[6] and northern Syria, regions that would generally become Aramean by the late second millennium B.C. Hundreds of Amorite personal names preserved in Akkadian texts also reveal the West Semitic roots of these newcomers to the Mesopotamian stage. Their languages were forms of Akkadian, an umbrella term that came to encompass various Semitic peoples of the ancient Near East, and their culture a blend of vigorous Semitic roots and older, refined Sumerian forms. Eventually the Amorites adopted the classic Babylonian dialect of Akkadian (Old Babylonian) for their correspondence, which was written, of course, in cuneiform.

It did not take long for this emerging Amorite presence to coalesce into two already-established power centers, one in Assyria along the upper Tigris River in northern Mesopotamia and the other in Babylon at the confluence of the Tigris and Euphrates in the south. Though often called the Old Assyrian and Old Babylonian Empires, respectively, Assyria and Babylon of the early second millennium B.C. are perhaps better seen as something less: the focal points of two widespread and somewhat insecure coalitions, each composed of several city- or nation-states linked by shared commercial, social and hence, political interests. The classic insider's view was that of Itur-Asdu, the ambassador of Zimri-Lim of Mari in Nahor, who wrote to his king during the reign of Hammurapi:

No king is truly powerful just on his own. Ten to fifteen kings follow

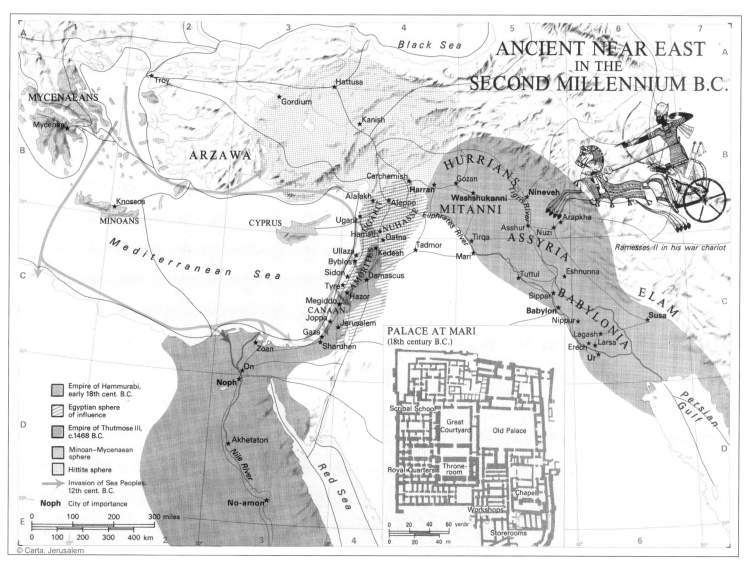

© Carta, Jerusalem

Hammurapi of Babylon receives the law from the sun god, Shamash; detail of his Code discovered at Susa.

Hammurapi of Babylon, Rim-Sin of Larsa, Ibal-pi-El of Eshnunna or Amut-pi-El of Qatna, but 20 kings follow Yarim-Lin of Yamhad.[7]

Itur-Asdu rightly gave Hammurapi pride of place as first in the list, but as a resident of Mari he favored the numerical superiority of a fellow westerner, Yarim-Lim of Yamhad, whose capital was at Aleppo. Economic interests at the time were regional, linked at least in part by a lively trade in metals (primarily copper and tin, which together make bronze), an international diplomatic corps and a literate, urban bureaucracy that tracked the movements of all. Visible in the official correspondence are treaties, foreign missions, marriage alliances, negotiations, ratifications, oaths of loyalty and the like, with petty local chieftains wanting to jump aboard. Throughout was an awareness of groups of tribal pastoralists (semi-nomadic sheep and goat herders) who tried to either participate in, or thwart, the urban network that was taking hold of the lands of the Tigris and Euphrates. F. M. Th. Boehl has called the whole thing "a period of armed peace."[8]

The most successful Assyrian version of such a coalition was headed by Shamshi-Adad, an Amorite general who usurped the throne of Asshur in c. 1813 B.C. From his capital at Shubat-Enlil northwest of Asshur, Shamshi-Adad controlled lands that reached westward along the great bend of the Euphrates. He placed his younger son Yasmah-Adad on the throne of Mari on the Middle Euphrates and his older son Ishme-Dagan as king at Ekallatum south of Asshur on the Upper Tigris. Though anticipating the kind of military efficiency that would dominate the Neo-Assyrian Empire in the first millennium B.C., this patriarchy of city-states was unable to defeat an emerging Babylonian coalition to the south (Babylon, Larsa and Eshnunna). The Assyrian coalition eventually fell apart after the death of Shamshi-Adad, when son Ishme-Dagan placed himself under the authority of the rising Hammurapi of Babylon.

Hammurapi was a charismatic personality who took full advantage of having come from a stable dynastic line (he was the sixth of eleven kings of a largely peaceful dynasty, the shortest rule of which was still a relatively long 14 years). Hammurapi himself reigned for 43 years (1792–1750 B.C.), and during his tenure as an enlightened despot managed to turn the little-known city of Babylon into the center of a secure and flourishing political world. Requisite battles to the south, northeast and west early in his reign (years 6–10) and again when he was older (regnal years 29–37) secured Babylonian territorial control from Uruk to Eshnunna to Mari; tenacious Assyria was never completely subdued. The years between were filled with various internal matters aimed at consolidating Hammurapi's growing kingdom (irrigation works, temple building and fortifications).

But the reputation by which Hammurapi will ever be remembered was forged through his vision of social reform. At the beginning of his reign Hammurapi issued a *misharum*, a formal pronouncement aimed at remedying various economic malfunctions in the kingdom that he had inherited. His reputation for fostering justice—at least as he wanted his subjects to believe he had done, based on the prologue and epilogue of his now famous Code—is renowned, and became the earliest template by which the social effectiveness of all other monarchs of the ancient Near East have been judged.[9] Many of the laws of the Code of Hammurapi place an emphasis on individual rights. That is, the Code recognized a category of people (the *awilum*) who had rights worth protecting even though they were not attached to the palace or temple. In this, Hammurapi fostered a social system that encouraged the rise of independent economic sub-units that could operate somewhat freely among established channels of power. This "private sector" had property rights and the right to use hired labor. Whether a cause or a result of policies such as these, Mesopotamia experienced a remarkable cultural flowering during the Old Babylonian Period, with an emphasis on literacy and a synthesis of religion under the supremacy of Marduk, the city-turned-national god of Babylon.[10]

The Babylonian bridge to the world of the biblical patriarchs was the city of Mari, on the Middle Euphrates. The gateway to the west, Mari was formally conquered by Hammurapi in 1759 B.C. The discovery of an archive of 25,000 documents in the remains of the 300-room palace of Zimri-Lim, king of Mari during the reigns of Shamshi-Adad and Hammurapi, has provided a wide-open window into living conditions in middle Mesopotamia and the northern Levant during the eighteenth century B.C.; indeed, it is our primary source of information for the Amorite Period. Of particular interest for the world of the biblical patriarchs, the Mari texts mention a complex interface between urban dwellers and semi-nomadic, pastoral tribes (e.g. the *Māre-Yamina*—"Sons of the South" and *Māre-Šim'al*—"Sons of the North," among others) that saw goods and services move between both, usually to the benefit of everyone. Moreover, from these texts we know that Mari's economic orbit reached southward as far as Dan and Hazor, cities that later became the northern gateways into the land of ancient Israel.[11] On the whole, we can see that in their personal names (e.g. *Ya'qub-el*), patterns of social organization and habits of lifestyle, the pastoralists mentioned in connection with the city of Mari remind us of the biblical patriarchs. A number of other textual corpuses from the late third and early second millennium have also been called upon to illustrate the lives of the patriarchs (e.g. Ebla, Nuzi, Alalkh, Ugarit, the Execration Texts), but the Mari texts remain special because of their chronological timeframe and nearer proximity to what would become the homeland of ancient Israel.

While the lands of the Levant south of Mari lay on the frontier of the Old Babylonian Empire—politically beyond the pale though certainly within reach of its economic interests—we can form an overall picture of the region as it was during the Middle Bronze Age from other sources. The archaeological record of the southern Levant during the time of the patriarchs—it wasn't to be called Canaan until somewhat later—paints a consistent picture: powerful, walled city-states operating independently yet with a clear awareness of each other, and the absence of direct political control by anyone from Mesopotamia. Although pastoralists like Abraham and his descendants left no archaeologically-recoverable material culture and so are invisible in the overall historical record of the time, we can safely assume that the city-states of the southern Levant entered into the same kind of symbiotic relationships with pastoralists in their vicinity that we see in the contemporary Mari texts. The band of steppe land separating the highlands of Palestine from open

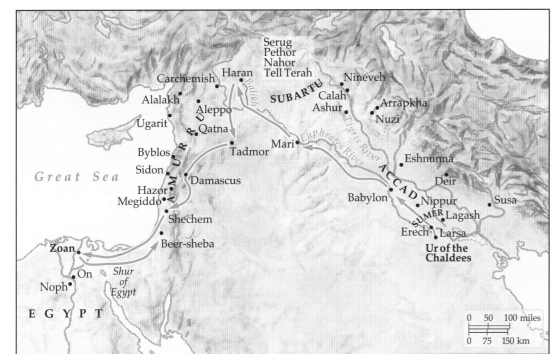

© Carta, Jerusalem

There was an Amorite presence in the southern Levant when Abraham got there (Gen 14:13) which persisted throughout the time of Joshua's conquest (Num 21:21–32; Josh 5:1; Judg 11:22; 1 Kgs 9:20), but the Bible is quite clear that Abraham and his family were something else, separate even from these Amorites who, with the Canaanites (cf. Gen 12:5-6), were the indigenous inhabitants of that land. So in a sense Abraham wasn't even at home in his new homeland but, as seasonally-moving pastoralists usually are, an outsider looking in (cf. Heb 11:8–12).

Like his contemporaries across the Fertile Crescent, Abraham and his family followed seasonal grazing lands from his home base at Beersheba in the Negeb, south into the open desert in good winters, then back up into the wetter hills during the long, dry months of summer (Gen 13:3; 14:13; 20:1; 37:12–17). In times of famine they made sure to stick close to the resources of an established city-state, either in the southern Levant or, if necessary, the Egyptian Delta (Gen 12:10; 26:1). Throughout this wide-ranging territory we can be sure that Abraham entered into formal, dimorphic (symbiotic, or mutually-beneficial) relationships with key city-states, at Shechem, Bethel, Hebron and Gerar. Realistically he would not have been allowed to build altars, plant crops or trees, dig wells and/or buy property, thus claiming permanency of place and its resources, otherwise (Gen 12:6–8; 20:1–18; 21:22-34; 23:1–20). Isaac had enough foresight to renew his father Abraham's relationships diplomatically (Gen 26:1–33); *his* son Jacob was more blunt, conquering Shechem and its favored location outright (Gen 34:1–31). The Mari texts, too, portray a prolonged and complicated process of give and take, encroachment and cooperation, mutual hostility and mutual need, between pastoralists and neighboring city-states,

desert to the east, which essentially follows the 12-inch rainfall line marking areas that were suitable for permanent agriculture from those where grazing was the only viable economic base, traces the entire arc of the Fertile Crescent from Babylon to Mari and down to places like Shechem, Bethel, Hebron and Gerar. It was along this length that we can reasonably place the movements of Abraham, Isaac, Jacob and Joseph, following the seasonal patterns of rainfall to graze their flocks and in the process sharing resources through symbiotic relationships with key city-states "in the land that I will show you" (Gen 12:1).

* * * * *

From Genesis to Ezekiel the biblical record recognizes that the origins of the patriarchs were in northwest Mesopotamia, where the Amorite presence was most dominant (Gen 11:31–32; 24:1–10; 29:1–14).[12] Haran, homeland of Abraham's extended family, was a large, sophisticated and profitable city-state on the Balih branch of the Euphrates northwest of Mari. Its name comes from the Akkadian word *harrānu* which means variously "highway," "crossroads," "journey," "caravan" or "business venture involving travel," and says something about the pastoral patriarch's favored resource base should he have decided to stay. "Your father was an Amorite," declared Ezekiel, reminding his Jerusalem audience of their patriarch's homeland origins (Ezek 16:3), while in a similar claim the author of Deuteronomy used the Late Bronze name for people of the same region: "My father was a wandering Aramean" (Deut 26:5; cf. Gen 31:24). Yet when Abraham is actually identified ethnically it is as neither an Amorite nor an Aramean but as a Hebrew (Gen 14:13), a descendant of Eber, someone earlier yet (Gen 10:21, 24–25; 11:16–17).

The closest photographs of an Abraham today are taken among shepherds who live in the arid hills of southern Israel or Jordan. Here they tend flocks of sheep and goats on rocky hillsides or along dry flats that lie within proximal distance of villages, but beyond the line where crops can predictably grow.

THE KINGS OF THE NORTH (GEN 14)

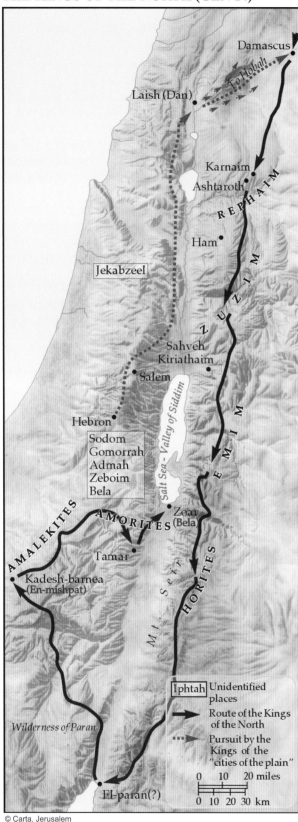

Damascus

To Hobah

Laish (Dan)

Karnaim
Ashtaroth

REPHAIM

Ham

Jekabzeel

ZUZIM

Sahveh
Kiriathaim

EMIM

Salem

Hebron

Sodom
Gomorrah
Admah
Zeboim
Bela

Salt Sea – Valley of Siddim

Zoar
(Bela)

Mt. Seir

AMALEKITES

AMORITES

HORITES

Tamar

Kadesh-barnea
(En-mishpat)

Wilderness of Paran

| Iphtah | Unidentified places |

➤ Route of the Kings of the North

┄┄➤ Pursuit by the Kings of the "cities of the plain"

0   10   20 miles

0 10 20 30 km

El-paran(?)

© Carta, Jerusalem

order to compel the latter's continued loyalty to the Mesopotamian cause.[13] Abraham got involved on the side of the five, exercising his expected role as protector of his family and their frontier. In this episode we read that Abraham's patriarchy, though without a proper heir, still included a large extended family of 318 men "born into his house," all old enough to fight on his behalf (Gen 14:14). To this we must add a proper proportion of women and children. As patriarch, Abraham was responsible for them all. The phrase "born into his house" indicates that each of the members of this formidable force were formally tied to Abraham "as sons," even though all had likely become attached to the patriarch through a variety of covenants that were forged and sealed on the individual level (anthropologists speak of "invented genealogies" that serve practical social purposes). One, Eliezar of Damascus, even served as Abraham's (temporary) heir (Gen 15:2–3). The need to forge alliances on every level is consistent with classic tribalism, the type of social organization in which Abraham and the pastoralists of the Mari texts certainly participated, with the details of who may have been allied to whom at any given moment remaining fluid.

Hospitality and cleverness, faithfulness and fluidity were all values necessary to survive in the Middle Bronze Age (they still are). On these accounts the biblical patriarchs participated fully in the larger world from which they were called, while at the same time standing as a people apart. The patriarchal narratives show a genuine awareness of place, and work with the assumption that the founding fathers of the Biblical record participated in the larger arenas of civilization that typically define the ancient Near East. Yet the Bible is also clear that the people of Israel-to-be were not one with them. *Their* priorities were no longer to be focused on the political, religious or economic interests of the established power bases in Mesopotamia (indeed, even Laban of Haran, Abraham's own nephew, become a foe; Gen 29:21–30; 30:25–43; 31:1–55), but on a new set of relationships in a land that lay very much on the Mesopotamian frontier. Simply put, Abraham and his emerging family were called to be distinct in a new land, covenanted to a God yet unknown to the peoples of the lands from which they had come. The encounter that would become Israel had begun.

A bedouin and his trusty guide, together with a student of biblical history (center), demonstrate the proper technique of slaughtering a sheep in Wadi Rum, Jordan. That there is life in the blood is obvious; guardians of sheep like the patriarch Abraham knew full well the price of animal sacrifice, and what the practice beheld for those wanting to approach God.

all fostered by skills of diplomacy, hospitality and survivalism ("being clever," one might say). In this way at least Abraham and his family were right at home in their new land on the Amorites' far southern frontier.

The tendency for city-states to form alliances with not only powerful pastoral clans in their vicinity but also each other, a pattern that characterized the age of Hammurapi, is well illustrated in the narrative of Genesis 14. Here four Mesopotamian kings join forces to fight five city-state kings in the vicinity of the Dead Sea in

The New Kingdom of Egypt and Israel's Exodus and Conquest of Canaan

Egypt had an advantage bestowed on it by geography that the homelands of the other great empires of the ancient Near East could only envy. Not only did the Delta and Nile Valley enjoy a high baseline of basic renewable resources,[14] Egypt was neatly isolated from the world around and so could grow and prosper in relative peace. Vast expanses of open desert to the west and east, a series of cataracts blocking river navigation from the south, and an overgrown, swampy delta to the north all conspired to give the ancient Egyptians a sense of security along the banks of their Nile. The Greek geographer Strabo said it succinctly: "Egypt is hard to enter."[15]

Yet there were ways in and out. Egypt's most important gateway (at least the one that is documented most frequently in ancient sources) lay to the northeast, across the Sinai and into the southern Levant, where it opened to the international land routes of Asia, Arabia and Europe. With an arid to hyper-arid landscape, the Sinai nearly proved too much for large armies from Mesopotamia or the Anatolian Plateau to cross, lying as it did at the very end of their already-stretched supply lines (until Egypt's encounter with Alexander in 331 B.C. occupations of Egyptian soil by foreign powers never seemed to take hold). But the Sinai was the *first* region crossed by an Egyptian army heading the other way, close enough so that the Pharaohs were able to establish and maintain a series of military way stations across its northern end (the "Horus Road") all the way to Gaza, Egypt's launch pad into Asia.[16] The doorway of the Sinai, then, opened most often to Egypt's favor, fostering in Egyptian consciousness a sense that although the southern Levant was foreign, it most naturally belonged to them.

Though Egypt's interaction with Asia peaked with the pharaohs of the New Kingdom in the second half of the second millennium B.C., it of course began much earlier. The discovery of semi-precious stones among grave goods in Pre-Dynastic Egyptian burials (the fourth millennium B.C.) attests to a vibrant trading activity with places as far afield as Afghanistan, prior to the unification of Egypt and even the invention of writing. Egypt's interests in the Levant during the third millennium B.C. (the Old Kingdom, or Age of the Pyramids) can be traced through the Negeb to Arad and up the coast as far as Byblos. The likely goal was to secure a supply of big timber, salt and bitumen, all commodities lacking along the Nile Valley, with the primary mechanism commercial, rather than military, ventures. This policy continued into the first half of the second millennium B.C. (Middle Kingdom Egypt), with the Execration Texts[17] (curses uttered on kings of cities in the southern Levant who tried to avoid their obligations to Egypt) our best textual witness to Egyptian control in the region. The Egyptian Pharaohs of the Middle Kingdom's Twelfth Dynasty thus maintained a structure of economic and administrative control over key cities in the southern Levant, though evidence of permanent military garrisons is lacking.

All of this changed with the rise of Egypt's New Kingdom, the Eighteenth and Nineteenth Dynasties (c. 1550–1186 B.C.). The catalyst was a period of weakness during the sixteenth century B.C. (the Second Intermediate Period; c. 1795–1550 B.C.), in which the central authority of the Pharaoh collapsed, formal political systems became fragmented and regular patterns of Egypt-initiated contact with the outside world, including trade relationships in the Levant, were reduced.

The seam between the eastern Delta and the Sinai has always been an open sieve. While formal armies had yet to penetrate the Horus Road by the time of the Middle Kingdom, the border was forever permeable by semi-nomads seeking easy grazing for their flocks, or sedentary peoples from the southern Levant who as simple settlers were attracted to the predictable supply of life-resources in Egypt. Illegal immigrants everywhere are tolerated at best, and usually met with suspicion. Abraham's temporary move into the Delta during a time of famine illustrates the reality here well (Gen 12:9–20). It was a geo-social dynamic that Egypt was helpless to prevent, and fed the opinion that foreigners were "not people one respects but wretches, craven-hearted"[18] as well as the attitude that "every shepherd is loathsome to the Egyptians" (Gen 46:34).

Enter the Hyksos, Semites from places on coastal and inland Canaan (for so the southern Levant can now be called) who, over time, infiltrated the eastern Delta in such numbers that they were able to wrest a degree of political control from the Egyptians (the Fifteenth Dynasty; c. 1650–1550 B.C.). Native Egyptians were shaken out of their complacency, for their game, at least in the eastern Delta, had been taken from them. It took about a century to turn back the tide; around the year 1560 B.C. Kamose and Ahmose, two brothers from the old Upper Egyptian political and religious center of Thebes, reunified Egypt and drove the Hyksos back across the Sinai.

Ancient Egypt was never the same. Having been conquered for the first time by foreigners, the Egyptians responded by crafting the hardware for an empire the likes of which the world had not yet seen. Front and center was the development of a permanent, professional army with standing garrisons in Egypt and their (re-)conquered territories, with specialized regiments of infantry and chariotry, lead by the crown prince and funded by a Pharaoh-centric

THE EXPULSION OF THE HYKSOS, 1560 B.C.

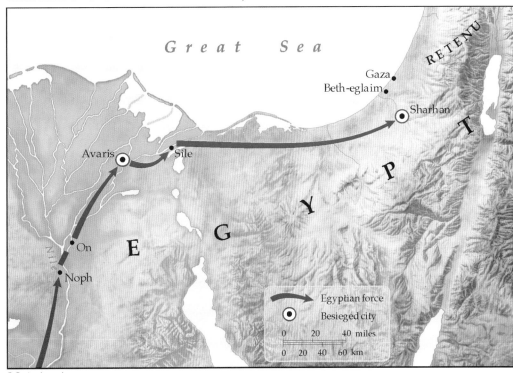

© Carta, Jerusalem

The strength of New Kingdom Egypt can be seen in the resolute pose of Rameses II, at the Luxor Temple.

perhaps the best known of all ancient Egyptian Pharaohs. With him, Egypt reached the height of its power and influence in the ancient Near East. The Egyptians considered the international corridors of Canaan—particularly the Coastal Plain, Jezreel Valley and Hulah Basin—necessary territories, with cities in the hill country above, notably Shechem and Jerusalem, needed to ensure highland loyalty.

For their part, the independent-minded Canaanite city-states seem to have tolerated the Egyptian presence in their land, knowing that they were no match for the world's most powerful army and, no doubt, profiting from the revenue that moved through anyway. Economically it was only a benefit to have the world's largest trading partner just a Sinai away. Yet independence is independence, and when the opportunity to push their own interests arose during the Amarna Age (albeit still under shadow of Egypt), various opportunistic Canaanite kings lost little time in testing their wings (Labay'u of Shechem comes immediately to mind). The point is that Egyptian suzerainty was no more welcome in Canaan than Canaanite infiltrators were in the Egyptian Delta, even though both could benefit economically from the presence of the other.

* * * * *

All of this brings us to Israel's experience in Egypt and the move from there back into Canaan, the land where patriarchal associations were wrapped in the promises of God (cf. Ex 6:2–8). Israel's actual experiences in Egypt prior to the Exodus were a mixed bag. On the one hand, the northeastern Delta (Goshen; Ex 8:22; 9:26), where the Hebrews lived, was a blessed and profitable land; this even the writers of the Bible recognized (cf. Gen 13:10: Deut 11:10). Though slaves, they were able to eat well (Ex 16:3; Num 11:4-5), own income-producing property (Ex 9:4, 6) and multiply and grow strong (Ex 1:20). Based on parallels to the community of Deir el-Medina in Upper Egypt, it is perhaps better to describe

levy on the general populace. (The Egyptians "borrowed" the harnessed horse and chariot, composite bow, chisel-shaped battle ax and ribbed dagger from the Hyksos, who had introduced this advanced military hardware to Egypt in the first place). The goal was to create a military buffer state in Canaan that would deflect invasion by other empires stirring on the northern horizon (initially Mitanni in northern Mesopotamia, then the Hittites in Anatolia), while providing a firm base of operations to take the battle to other peoples' lands. Of course the world's economy would bend to the pharaohs in the process, supported in part by Egypt's monopoly on Nubian gold brought down the Nile from the south.

The next four centuries were a time of heady nationalism and triumph for Egypt in Asia. Pharaoh after New Kingdom Pharaoh led military campaigns along the Horus Road to Gaza, then north the length of the Coastal Plain to Megiddo. From there Egypt had options: northwest to Acco, southeast to Beth-shean or farther north past Hazor to Damascus and Kadesh on the Orontes, in the northern Levant.[19] Together, this was the basic pattern of march, and by establishing permanent garrisons at key cities on these routes Egypt was able to effectively control Canaan throughout the New Kingdom (Canaan's Late Bronze Age; 1550–1200 B.C.). Pharaohs of note from the Eighteenth Dynasty include Thutmose III (1479–1425) and his son Amenhotep II (1427–1400), who pushed through Canaan on their way to check the Mitanni threat in the far north, and Amenhotep III (1390–1352), who reaped the benefit of his predecessors' efforts. This was a true international age, with Mitanni, the Hittites, Assyria, Babylon and Alashia (Cyprus) all vying for position and the right to be the favorite trading partner of Egypt.

Egypt's influence in Canaan waned somewhat during the reign of Amenhotep IV–Akhenaten (1352–1336; the el-Amarna Age), as various cities in Canaan took advantage of a period of Egyptian introspection to exert their own interests at the expense of their Nile overlord, and each other. But a revival of militaristic energy under the family of the Ramesides brought Egypt back into Asia with a vengeance. The Nineteenth Dynasty pharaohs Seti I (1294–1279), Rameses II (1279–1213) and Mernepthah (1213–1203) all campaigned in Canaan, with Rameses II, due to a reign of 67 years and, no doubt, a personality most worthy of triumphalistic Egypt,

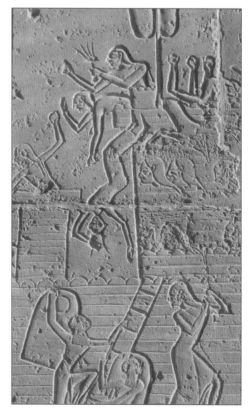

The Egyptian army of Rameses II assaults the Canaanite stronghold of Kedesh on the Orontes in an image from the Ramesseum in Upper Egypt.

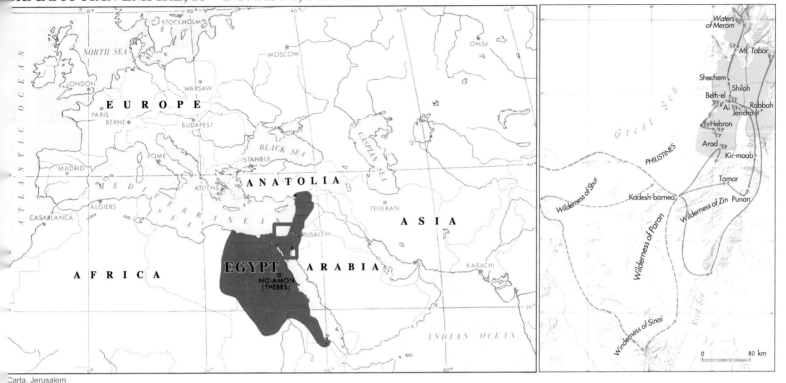

Israel's experience in Egypt as a kind of permanent *corvée* on behalf of the Pharaoh.[20] On the other hand, whatever advantages living in Egypt might initially have held for ancient Israel, these did not outweigh the reality of the Egyptian attitude toward foreigners, nor Egypt's tendency to subjugate outsiders lest they try to replay the "Hyksos card," or Israel's realization that while slaving away for the Pharaoh may have been acceptable had they been native Egyptians, the projects on which they were working weren't theirs. This land just wasn't where Israel belonged.

The mention of Israelite work on two east Delta royal cities, Pithom and Rameses, in Exodus 1:11 suggests that Israel's Exodus from Egypt took place sometime during the reign of Rameses II, when Egyptian authority in Canaan was at its height. Crossing the Red Sea with an entire people in tow for a homeland they had not yet seen, Moses recognized that the Egyptian military presence on the Horus Road ("the way to the land of the Philistines;" Ex 13:17) was too strong and so turned southward instead, toward the southern end of the Peninsula and Mount Sinai, an area of refuge and escape. From there it was a 40-year, circuitous journey in and around the harshest part of the Sinai (an area now called *et-Tih*, "the One Who is Lost"), like their patriarchal ancestors following the seasons of available grass from oasis to available watering hole (and sometimes there were none). And as long as Israel remained in the Sinai, in a middle-land between Egypt and Canaan, the resources of the eastern Delta stayed in their collective memory, a magnet pulling them back to a life that at least had been sustainable ("We remember the fish we used to eat for free in Egypt, the cucumbers, the melons, the leeks and the garlic" Num 11:4-5; cf. Ex 16:3).

Fair enough. But once Israel entered Canaan, Egypt left their radar screen completely. The actual footprint of Egypt in Canaan had not changed; its impress was just completely ignored in the biblical account of the conquest and early settlement of Israel (the books of Joshua and Judges). Biblical historians have debated all sides of the point, but the plain sense seems easy enough: now that Israel was back home, the long arm of Egypt was simply no longer relevant.

In a victory poem dated to his fifth regnal year (c. 1207 B.C.), Mernepthah, son and successor of Rameses II, mentions that he encountered and defeated a people group in Canaan called "Israel."[21] This is clear evidence that Israel had not only entered Canaan but was already a force worth reckoning with by that time. The sequence of battles that prompted Mernepthah's account—and it must have been significant as this is the first and only time the name Israel appears in ancient Egyptian texts—is nowhere mentioned in the Bible.[22] What the conquest and early settlement accounts do mention is a series of struggles—some full battles (e.g. against Jericho, Ai and Hazor; Joshua 6–8, 11), others infiltration, expansion and holding one's own (e.g. Josh 17:14–18 and the episodes of Judges). The enemies here were indigenous Canaanites and Amorites, as well as any number of other people groups such as the Philistines who were in the process of gaining a foothold in this or that pocket of Canaan as well. The book of Joshua provides a "map" of Canaan in which the entire land lying between the Mediterranean and the Jordan River, "from Dan to Beer-sheba," was apportioned to Israel. Yet the "map" of the book of Judges shows that while Israel indeed made settlement progress in the hills, their various tribes were not able to move onto the coastal plain or into Canaan's large inland valleys. It was here, we read, where the Canaanite strongholds could be found, large cities with chariots of iron (Josh 11:4; Judg 1:19; 4:3). The Egyptians, charioteers in their own right, had their strongholds in exactly the same place, but as we have seen, the biblical writers had no reason to mention *that* (to admit that they fled Egypt only to the Egyptian army well ensconced in their new homeland was a bit too much).

And so Israel first settled the empty parts of the Land Between. There would come a time, much later, during the monarchy when Israel and Judah had grown strong and lived securely in their homeland, that Egypt could be mentioned by the prophets and courted by the kings, but that was later. For now, Egypt was a thing of the past. And with the prohibition of making graven images, even the Egyptian hieroglyphic writing system, let alone everything that it stood for, was eschewed.

Egypt's Waning Empire and the Rise of Kingship in Israel

As dominant as Egypt had been in Canaan during the Late Bronze Age (1550–1200 B.C.), it eventually went the way of all empires. The decline was rapid: within half a century of its greatest success (Rameses II's peace treaty with the Hittites in 1258 B.C.), Gaza and the southern coastal plain had fallen to the Philistines and, cut off at the pass, Egypt's influence in Canaan foundered. Egypt's magnificent Nineteenth Dynasty barely survived the death of its greatest pharaoh. A contributing cause was perhaps Rameses II's unusually long reign: at 67 years, "complacency" outpaced "stability." Rameses outlived his first eight crown princes, and while son number nine, Merneptah, was able to hold the line in Canaan, the inexorable digress to dynastic instability had set in.

Six pharaohs and nineteen years later, power was finally solidified under the personage of Rameses III (1184–1153 B.C.), of Dynasty Twenty. This Rameses modeled himself after his namesake ("III" took the same throne names as "II," and gave many of his sons the same names his more illustrious predecessor did his). But shows of personal and national protocol were not enough. It was one of those periods of time in world history when, as seen through the privilege of hindsight, the very foundations of the civilized world were shaken. Great movements of people and momentous changes in the makeup of nations can be traced from the Aegean to Mesopotamia and down into Egypt at the end of the thirteenth and beginning of the twelfth centuries B.C. Rameses III happened to be in the wrong place at the wrong time.

For Egypt the sequence was familiar enough, but this time it was an end-game. In his fifth year and again in his eleventh, Rameses III drove Libyans out of the western Delta (like the earlier Hyksos problem in the eastern Delta, the Libyans had a habit of becoming too comfortable within the folds of Egypt territory and ended up clamoring too loudly for political control). In his eighth year (1176 B.C.), between these thrusts, Rameses III tried to do the same with Sea Peoples.

"Sea Peoples" is a generic term for a loosely related group (or groups) of Indo-Europeans hailing from the Aegean (cf. Amos 9:7; Jer 47:4) and Anatolia who had been making their way toward the southeastern bend of the Mediterranean, by land and by sea, since at least the mid-thirteenth century B.C. The causes of their migration are debated and ultimately unknowable, but likely were related to instability and population pressure in Greece. Egyptian sources identify several groups of Sea Peoples who pushed into the outlets of the Nile and southern Levant: the Weshesh, Shekelesh, Denyen (a name reminiscent of the biblical tribe of Dan, whose initial tribal territory was in the vicinity of Joppa; Josh 19:40–48), Sicels (who are seen around Acco and Dor) and Peleshet, the Philistines of the biblical record.[23]

In one of the greatest attempts of face-saving propaganda from the ancient world, Rameses III reported that he defeated the Sea Peoples in pitched battle, then "allowed" them to settle on Canaan's southern coast. In reality, the Philistine presence at Gaza by the mid-twelfth century B.C. signaled the end of continued Egyptian dominance in Canaan. One must assume that the Egyptian garrisons in Megiddo and Beth-shean were withdrawn, and that Egyptian influence in the ports of Phoenicia—a fact of life that had defined the economy of the ancient Near East for two millennia—was severely curtailed. The folksy Egyptian *Tale of Wen-Amun* speaks of the troubles faced by Wen-Amon, an official from the Amun Temple in Karnak, when he journeyed to Phoenicia in order to purchase wood for the construction of the sacred solar boat belonging to Amun, Egypt's all-powerful national deity. Robbed by the Sicels, disrespected and left without recourse in Phoenicia by authorities formerly loyal to Egypt, then chased to Alashia (Elishah; mod. Cyprus) where he was attacked again, Wen-Amon's official ties meant nothing.[24] Egyptian pride could scarcely come to terms with the new world order.

With a broken economy fueling unrest at home, Egyptian sources suggest that the unthinkable happened: dissatisfied and disillusioned forces back home assassinated Rameses III, their divine Pharaoh. The rest of the Twentieth Dynasty was filled with a quick succession of wholly unremarkable pharaohs (Rameses IV–XI; 1184–1069 B.C.), and with them Egypt slid into economic stagnation, political unrest and the malaise of the Third Intermediate Period. The emerging nation-states of Canaan couldn't have been more pleased.

But Egypt possessed too grand a history of success in the southern Levant to be so easily stayed. The age of successive pharaohs launching multiple campaigns into Canaan may have been over, but the resources of the Nile were still rich enough to allow individual pharaohs, when political conditions were aligned, the wherewithal for single thrusts into the southern Levant. This happened every cou-

THE MIGRATION OF THE SEA PEOPLES, 1174 B.C.

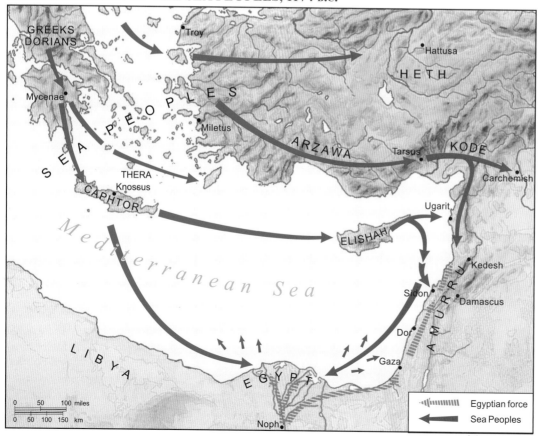

© Carta, Jerusalem

THE TRAVELS OF WEN-AMON

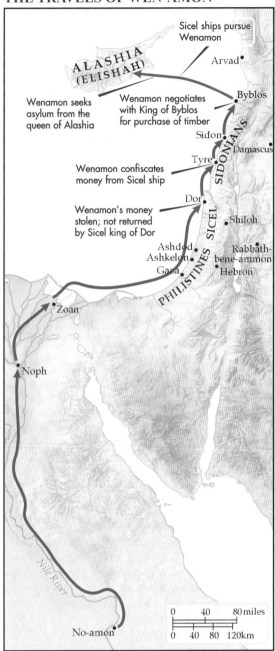

Sicel ships pursue Wenamon

ALASHIA (ELISHAH)

Arvad

Wenamon seeks asylum from the queen of Alashia

Wenamon negotiates with King of Byblos for purchase of timber

Byblos

Sidon

Damascus

SIDONIANS

Tyre

Wenamon confiscates money from Sicel ship

Dor

Wenamon's money stolen; not returned by Sicel king of Dor

SICEL

Shiloh

PHILISTINES

Ashdod
Ashkelon
Gaza

Rabbath-bene-ammon
Hebron

Zoan

Noph

Nile River

No-amon

| 0 | 40 | 80 miles |
| 0 | 40 | 80 | 120km |

© Carta, Jerusalem

in the biblical text), while the third was an attempt at check-mating Israel by Shishak (c. 945–924 B.C.), two pharaohs later.

It started with Hadad, a ranking member of the royal house of Edom, who fled to Egypt after David had conquered his homeland. There Hadad was well received, wined and dined and married into the Egyptian royal line with Siamun's hope, apparently, that when the situation presented itself, Hadad (or his son) would assume the Edomite throne a loyal Egyptian lackey (1 Kgs 11:14–22). Ditto with Jeroboam, an able and ambitious fellow in charge of Solomon's *corvée* labor in the central hill country of Israel (the territory of Ephraim and Manasseh). With an eye on the kingship, Jeroboam, too, fled to Egypt and was, no doubt, received similarly (1 Kgs 11:26–40).

With prospective allies from lands on either side of Jerusalem in his pocket,

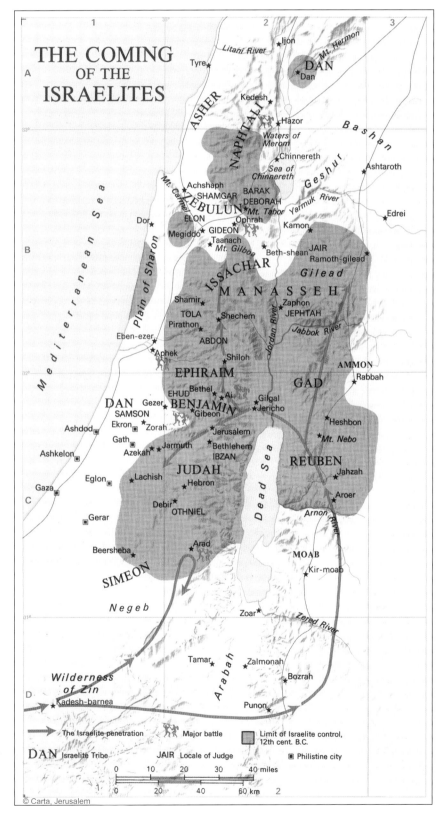

THE COMING OF THE ISRAELITES

Litani River
Ijon
Tyre
Mt. Hermon
DAN
Dan
ASHER
Kedesh
NAPHTALI
Hazor
Bashan
Waters of Merom
Chinnereth
Sea of Chinnereth
Geshur
Ashtaroth
Mt. Carmel
Achshaph
SHAMGAR
BARAK
DEBORAH
Yarmuk River
ZEBULUN
Mt. Tabor
Ophrah
Edrei
ELON
Dor
Megiddo
GIDEON
Kamon
Taanach
Mt. Gilboa
Beth-shean
JAIR
Ramoth-gilead
Mediterranean Sea
ISSACHAR
Gilead
MANASSEH
Plain of Sharon
Shamir
Zaphon
TOLA
Shechem
JEPHTAH
Pirathon
Jabbok River
Eben-ezer
ABDON
Aphek
Shiloh
AMMON
EPHRAIM
GAD
Rabbah
EHUD
Bethel
Ai
Gilgal
DAN
Gezer
BENJAMIN
Jericho
Heshbon
SAMSON
Gibeon
Ekron
Zorah
Mt. Nebo
Ashdod
Jerusalem
Gath
Bethlehem
REUBEN
Ashkelon
Azekah
Jarmuth
IBZAN
Jahzah
Eglon
Lachish
JUDAH
Dead Sea
Gaza
Hebron
Aroer
Debir
OTHNIEL
Arnon River
Gerar
MOAB
Beersheba
Arad
Kir-moab
SIMEON
Zoar
Zered River
Negeb
Tamar
Zalmonah
Wilderness of Zin
Bozrah
Kadesh-barnea
Arabah
Punon
Jordan River

→ The Israelite penetration   ⚔ Major battle   ▨ Limit of Israelite control, 12th cent. B.C.

DAN Israelite Tribe   **JAIR** Locale of Judge   ◼ Philistine city

| 0 | 10 | 20 | 30 | 40 miles |
| 0 | 20 | 40 | 60 km |

© Carta, Jerusalem

ple of generations or so, not frequently enough to kick-start the Egyptian Empire but enough to keep the kings of Canaan, especially Israel and Judah, on their toes.

With an entrenched Philistine presence on the south Levantine coast and the rise of David and Solomon's hill country kingdom spilling into the Jezreel Valley and Transjordan beyond, Egypt had to change its approach in Asia. The strongest of the pharaohs seem to have adopted a policy of currying favors with their former vassal city-states on the one hand, while using willing locals (or, unwitting collaborators?) to try to destabilize the emerging nation-states in Canaan on the other. Egypt's goal of course was to return to the level of power that it had enjoyed in Canaan during the New Kingdom, though in the end this was unachievable. In this regard three series of events corresponding with the rise of kingship in early Israel must be mentioned. The first two were set-up episodes and likely involved Siamun (c. 978–959 B.C.), pharaoh during the latter part of the reign of David and the early reign of Solomon (his name is not mentioned

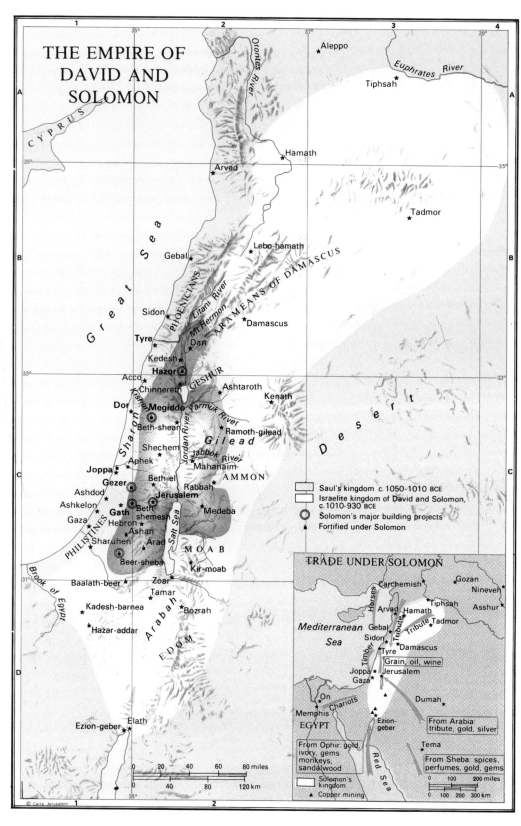

THE EMPIRE OF DAVID AND SOLOMON

CYPRUS

Great Sea

Orontes River

Aleppo

Euphrates River

Tiphsah

Hamath

Arvad

Tadmor

Lebo-hamath

Gebal

PHOENICIANS

Litani River

Mt. Hermon

ARAMEANS OF DAMASCUS

Sidon

Tyre

Dan

Damascus

Kedesh

Hazor

GESHUR

Acco

Chinnereth

Ashtaroth

Kenath

Dor

Megiddo

Yarmuk River

Beth-shean

Jordan River

Ramoth-gilead

Gilead

Shechem

Jabbok River

Aphek

Mahanaim

AMMON

Joppa

Beth-el

Gezer

Rabbah

Ashdod

Jerusalem

Ashkelon

Gath

Beth-shemesh

Medeba

Gaza

Hebron

PHILISTINES

Ashan

Sharuhen

Arad

Salt Sea

MOAB

Beer-sheba

Kir-moab

Baalath-beer

Zoar

Tamar

Brook of Egypt

Kadesh-barnea

Bozrah

Hazar-addar

Arabah

EDOM

Ezion-geber

Elath

Desert

Sharon

Kishon River

	Saul's kingdom c. 1050–1010 BCE
	Israelite kingdom of David and Solomon, c. 1010–930 BCE
◎	Solomon's major building projects
■	Fortified under Solomon

0 20 40 60 80 miles
0 40 80 120 km

© Carta, Jerusalem

TRADE UNDER SOLOMON

Mediterranean Sea

Carchemish

Gozan

Nineveh

Arvad

Hamath

Asshur

Tiphsah

Horses

Gebal

Tribute

Tadmor

Sidon

Timber

Tribute

Tyre

Damascus

Grain, oil, wine

Joppa

Jerusalem

Gaza

Dumah

On

Chariots

Memphis

EGYPT

Ezion-geber

From Arabia: tribute, gold, silver

Tema

From Ophir: gold, ivory, gems, monkeys, sandalwood

From Sheba: spices, perfumes, gold, gems

Red Sea

| | Solomon's kingdom |
| ▲ | Copper mining |

0 100 200 miles
0 100 200 300 km

---

advantage of a rapidly dividing kingdom in Israel, Shishak drove his army through the southern Levant in 930 B.C. A reasonable line of march can be reconstructed from the list of conquered cities that he had engraved on the outside wall of the Hypostyle Hall of the great Amun Temple in Karnak: across the Sinai to Gaza, through the Negeb toward Edom; up the coast to Gezer and into the hills north of Jerusalem, then gutting the central and northern hill country before parading through the Jezreel Valley and back home.[25] It was a "wake-up" call showing that Jeroboam had been a bit of a dupe. While Shishak's list of conquered cities doesn't include Jerusalem, the biblical account emphasizes Rehoboam's submission to the Egyptian pharaoh (1 Kgs 14:25–28; 2 Chron 12:1–12). This was to be Shishak's only campaign into the Levant, and the last of any Pharaoh for some time, but it was enough to give definitive shape to the reality that the nation-states of Canaan were not to develop into a united force that would permanently shut Egypt out.

*   *   *   *   *

The kings of Israel, of course, saw the situation developing differently. The Israelite tribes, largely confined to the Canaanite hill country in the days of the Judges (cf. Judg 1:27–36), slowly gained strength in terms of economy and numbers. Politically, the prompt to kingship was a series of conflicts with the Philistines; that Egypt had withdrawn from the coastal plain gave David in particular a green light to try to fill the imperial void. Most of David's recorded campaigns were against similar tribal kingdoms in Transjordan (Edom, Moab, Ammon, Aram-Damascus and, in the far north, Aram-Zobah). Yet all historical-geographical logic suggests that he was also able to bring the unconquered Canaanite cities on the coast and in the Jezreel Valley into the Israelite fold (2 Sam 8:1–15; 10:1–12:31;

Siamun made a move on the Philistine coast, Egypt's most essential region of Canaan. The Bible notes that pharaoh captured Gezer from the Canaanites and burned the city; by implication, the Philistine pentapolis (Ekron, Gath, Ashdod, Ashkelon and especially Gaza; cf. 1 Sam 6:17) must have fallen under a measure of Egyptian suzerainty as well. Recognizing Solomon's relative strength in the area, Siamun then entered into a marriage alliance with the Israelite king, apparently under the assumption that each monarch would protect the interests of the other on the coast, while trying to advance his own in the process (1 Kgs 9:16).

What may have looked like a favorable and permanent arrangement to Solomon fell apart as soon as the Israelite king died. Taking

cf. Judg 1:27–36). These included places which had had standing Egyptian garrisons such as Beth-shean, Rehob, Megiddo and Acco. Philistia, as well as the Aramean city-states further north, accepted David's suzerainty and their heads—many were emerging tribal leaders such as himself—became his vassal kings. The result was that David and Solomon "had dominion over everything west of the [Euphrates] River, from Tiphsah to Gaza, over all the kings west of the River" (1 Kgs 4:24). For the writer of Kings, God's promise that Abraham' descendants would have a land of their own had been fulfilled (cf. Gen 15:17–21).

David was the conquering hero; Solomon the Renaissance man under whom the kingdom thrived. But the Ghost of Egypt Present

Reconstructed remains of the New Kingdom Egyptian palace at Beth-shean attest to the imprint that pharaohs such as Seti I and Rameses II placed deep into Canaan. This site fell to the Israelite Kingdom in the days of Solomon.

was coming back alive, and Solomon knew that Israel's viability on the world stage couldn't ignore its larger neighbor across the Sinai. As long as David was alive the Philistines and Egypt were both shackled down on the coast. But as soon as he died, Egypt made a move, partly to check their old nemesis the Philistines (and reverse the earlier shame suffered under Rameses III), but partly to come to terms with Israel. Gezer guarded the best natural route between Jerusalem and the coast, via the cities of Lower and Upper Beth-horon and the Aijalon Valley, and Siamun knew that if he could not conquer Israel, he could at least position himself so that Solomon had to take him into account. It was to be an economic win-win for both, sealed by a political marriage of convenience (1 Kgs 9:16).

Solomon promptly fortified three key cities on the same imperial highway that connected Egypt with the northern Levant, thus assuring that he had access to both: Hazor, the gateway north; Megiddo, the center of the crossroads of the Jezreel Valley, and Gezer, the front door to Jerusalem (1 Kgs 9:15). He also fortified the Gezer-Jerusalem highway, his link to the world beyond, as well as Tamar, an oasis in the Rift Valley south of the Dead Sea that supplied the Jerusalem–Red Sea route as well as the natural highway linking Egypt with Edom and Arabia (1 Kgs 9:17).

Solomon now controlled exactly the same economic corridors in the southern Levant that historically had been dominated by Egypt. Fittingly, his rule also "looked" Egyptian. It was Solomon who garrisoned divisions of chariots and horsemen in chariot cities on the international highway. It was Solomon who brokered the lucrative trade in horses and chariots between Egypt and Kue (Cilicia), on the northern bend of the Mediterranean. It was Solomon who forged a trade alliance with the kings of Phoenicia, bringing timber to royal and temple building projects in Jerusalem. And it was Solomon who was able to tap into the shipping lanes of the Red Sea, pulling up gold and exotic goods from Africa and bypassing Egypt in the process (1 Kgs 9:26–10:29). The visit of the Queen of Sheba to Jerusalem is reminiscent of the visit of the Queen of Punt to Pharaoh Hatshepsut in the fifteenth century B.C., at the dawn of Egypt's New Kingdom. Solomon surely felt as though he stood at the brink of the same. Yet for all of Solomon's accomplishments we must not suppose that Israel had a complete monopoly on international trade in the southern Levant, since the arrangements with Siamun at Gezer suggest something of a partnership (1 Kgs

9:16). At the same time, because this is the only known instance of an Egyptian queen marrying a foreigner and taking up residence in *his* home, rather than he moving to Egypt, we can safely assume something about the relative strength of Solomon's Kingdom vis-à-vis Egypt at the time.

Other aspects of Solomon's reign also looked Egyptian. The practice of co-regencies by which a reigning monarch's chosen son exercised certain royal prerogatives had affinities with the Egyptian practice of placing the crown prince over the army (it was adopted in Jerusalem but not the Northern Kingdom). The division of Solomon's kingdom into twelve districts for taxation and his system of national *corvée* based on geographical districts was similar to the system of taxation used by Shishak (1 Kgs 4:1–19). In literature and world view, too, Solomon's kingdom echoed Egypt (though not of course its polytheism). "Solomon's wisdom surpassed the wisdom of all the sons of the east and all the wisdom of Egypt," the writer of Kings was pleased to note (1 Kgs 4:30-34), and wisdom literature attributed to him in the Bible (e.g. Proverbs 22–24; cf. 1 Kgs 4:32–33; Prov 1:1) bears similarities to *The Instruction of Amen-em-opet*, an Egyptian composition of the New Kingdom of the Third Intermediate Period.[26]

But Israel's Golden Age barely outlived its founders. Causes for the fall of the United Kingdom are many, but apparently centered on internal revolts and dynastic instability, the same factors of destruction that can be tracked in Egypt's own Intermediate Periods. Solomon's son Rehoboam built a series of fortresses to defend the most critical routes and strategic crossroads leading into the hill country of Judah, leaving the outer foothills, the coastal plain, the Negeb, the north and everything beyond to the easy grasp of Egypt (2 Chron 11:5–12). Though we don't know if Rehoboam built his network of fortifications in anticipation of Shishak's ripping attack through Israel and Judah or as a gut-check result, the two must have been related.

In the end Shishak couldn't follow up on his conquests, but neither could Rehoboam take advantage of the opportunity handed him when Egypt again withdrew. Internally, the Levant fell back into the role to which it was most accustomed: a number of small nation-states, each clinging to its own place, competing against each other for the resources of home. At least there would be another two centuries before the empire-vultures circling the horizon—this time in the form of Assyria—would swoop in again.

The six-chambered gate at Gezer, facing the hill country of Judah, reflects Solomon's hold on the city and his ability to use it as a launchpad for Jerusalem to the wealth of the coast.

The Assyrian Empire and Israel's Divided Kingdom

Assyria was the first of the great pan-Mesopotamian empires of the ancient world, and the first to overrun the kingdoms of Israel and Judah. Assyria's strike into the southern Levant hit with brute force in the late eighth century B.C., during the reigns Ahaz and Hezekiah and under the penetrating vision of Micah and Isaiah, prophets with a cause. The collision left an indelible mark on the historical and theological consciousness of ancient Israel.

The process of empire-building in Mesopotamia during the second millennium B.C. started with forced confederations of nation states (the Old Babylonian Period) then moved to the direct control of vassal states through the centralized rule of conquering kings (e.g. Mitanni, the Hittites, Hurrians, Kassites and even the Egyptians). All this culminated in the mid-first millennium B.C. as Assyria pursued policies which can best be described as colonial and imperialistic. Bent on economic and territorial expansion, the Assyrian kings imposed political and economic structures on peoples they conquered to ensure a constant shift of wealth (including manpower) from their continually expanding frontier back to the center (to the capital cities of Asshur, Calah/Nimrud, Dur-Sharruken/Khorsabad and Nineveh). Tiglath-pileser III (744–727 B.C.), who conquered Galilee in 733 B.C., tightened the noose by introducing the policy of creating Assyrian provinces out of rebellious vassal states, formally incorporating them into his empire. He then deported the indigenous leaders from these newly conquered lands to places deep within the empire and repopulated their cities with foreigners from elsewhere (cf. 2 Kgs 17:6, 24; 18:11; Isa 20:3–6). This practice was aimed at breaking down ideologically active regional centers (e.g. local palaces and temples that quite naturally resisted Assyrian control) and smoothing the Empire into

a quiescent, Assyro-Aramean mass, hopefully clipping the tendency for partisan revolt in the process (cf. 2 Kgs 17:24–41).

All of this presupposes a spirit of military aggressiveness, sanctioned by the Assyrian national god Asshur and fostered by ambitious kings. In order to supply the insatiable economic appetite of the empire's great organizations (temple and palace), the priests conveniently declared that Asshur had issued a decree to enlarge the frontiers of his empire.[27] War booty was considered tribute to the god, with the king standing in as Asshur's most capable agent. Justified by a theology of holy war, the Assyrian war machine became remarkably efficient: large armies powered by sophisticated means of transport were able to move long distances on a regular basis, while disciplined soldiers brandishing advanced weaponry perfected battle techniques (including siege warfare) that consumed, like a line of advancing fire, everything in their path. All of this was accompanied by a wave of propaganda, spread by speech (e.g. 2 Kgs 18:17–37), symbol (e.g. victory stela) and reality (e.g. the survivors of conquered cities such as Lachish were impaled on stakes and set before their smoldering city to induce the neighbors to surrender).[28] This "calculated frightfulness" (in the words of A. T. Olmstead[29]) was appallingly effective and sent shock waves across the expanding Assyrian frontier. Even so, not all local kings were so quickly cowed, and the fringes of the empire seethed in a constant state of revolt.

Although Assyria's encounters with Israel—and hence the focus of the biblical account—took place on the southwestern fringe of their empire, perspective can be gained by taking into account all three of Assyria's expanding frontiers. The rugged north and east, facing the Zagros Mountains and the highlands of Urartu and Per-

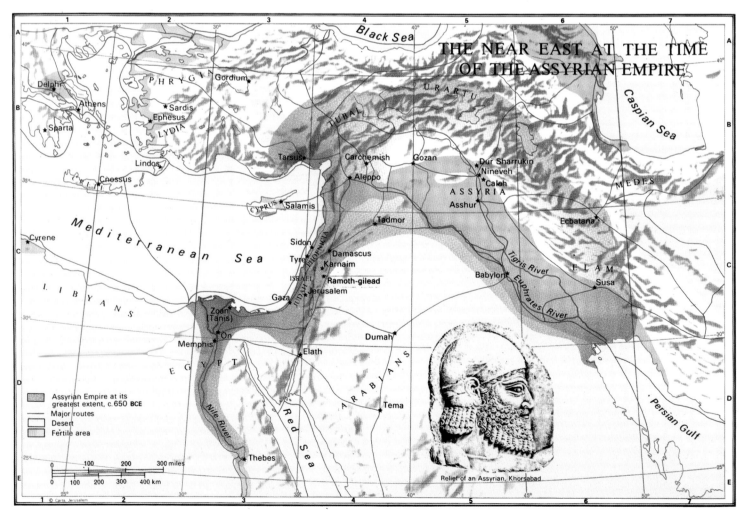

THE NEAR EAST AT THE TIME OF THE ASSYRIAN EMPIRE

Assyrian Empire at its greatest extent, c.650 BCE
Major routes
Desert
Fertile area

0   100   200   300 miles
0   100   200   300   400 km

© Carta, Jerusalem

Relief of an Assyrian, Khorsabad

sia, was a perpetual line of conflict. Here Assyria tried to create a series of small buffer-states that could hold back the mountainous hordes. Sargon II (721–705 B.C.), who had conquered the Philistine Coastal Plain (cf. Isa 20:1), fell in battle fighting the Cimmerians in the mountains of eastern Anatolia. His body was not recovered—it was considered an omen that the gods disfavored his reign—and revolt flared everywhere, including in Hezekiah's Judah. To the south, Babylon remained a bitter rival of Assyria even though these two ancient centers of Mesopotamian culture shared a common cuneiform civilization. Merodach-Baladan of Babylon was thus a natural ally of Hezekiah, as both tried to come to terms with the hammer blows of the Assyrian war machine (2 Kgs 20:12–15; Isa 39:1–8). But the focus of Assyria's imperialistic efforts was to the west, across the Euphrates to the Mediterranean and, eventually, into the deep-pocket wealth of Egypt. The small nation states of the Levant that lay between, including Aram-Damascus, Ammon, Phoenicia, Philistia, Israel and Judah, were so much road kill in the process.

The first Assyrian push westward was by Adad-nirari I (1305–1274 B.C.), who reached Carchemish on the Upper Euphrates. Coming just before the height of Egypt's conflict with the Hittites under Rameses II, this was perhaps a move to drive a wedge between the two great western powers through the heart of the recently collapsed Mitanni Empire and reach the northern Levant first. Neither Adad-nirari nor his successors could follow up, however, though Tiglath-pileser I (1114–1076 B.C.) did manage to reach Tadmor, commanding the more direct steppe-land route south of the Euphrates. For the next two centuries Assyria caved-in on itself, leaving a window of opportunity for local nationalist movements to establish a string of Aramean city states in the northern Levant (a corresponding withdrawal of Egypt in the south provided opportunity for Israel and its neighbors to establish themselves as independent nation states at the same time).

All this changed with the rise of Ashurnasirpal II (883–859 B.C.), whose calculated frightfulness ripped westward across the Euphrates, reached the "Upper Sea" (the Mediterranean) in c. 875 B.C., and demanded tribute from the city states of the northern Levant.[30] His successor Shalmaneser III (858–824 B.C.) pushed as far south as Damascus but didn't conquer the city. Hadad-ezer, king of Damascus, responded by leading a coalition of Levantine states (in which Israel's Ahab played a major role) against the Assyrians. He managed to stop them at Qarqar on the Orontes in 853 B.C.. The battle was nevertheless a turning point for Assyria (Qarqar was literally around the corner on their west then southern line of march), and set the stage for a series of hammer blows down into the Levant. Softening thrusts in 849, 848 and 845 B.C. were followed by a deep strike in 841 B.C., in which Shalmaneser III defeated Hazael, the new king of Damascus, at Mount Senir (Mount Hermon; Damascus itself held out). Shalmaneser also conquered several cities to the south and west of Hermon, including, likely, Hazor, before setting up a victory statue on "Baali-rasi," likely Mount Carmel. Adad-nirari III (810–783 B.C.) followed up by reaching the Mediterranean (802 B.C.) and Damascus (796 B.C.) before internal revolts led to a period of decline. The West enjoyed one last moment of calm.

But not for long. Under Tiglath-pileser III (746–727 B.C.) the Assyrians returned to the Levant with a vengeance (cf. 2 Kgs 15:19; his Babylonian name was Pul). Tiglath-pileser ushered in the real hey-day of Assyrian dominance over the West. A quick succession of campaigns—down the Phoenician and Philistine coasts (734 B.C.), through Galilee to Megiddo (733 B.C.) and finally capturing Damascus and Bashan (732 B.C.) draped a dark mantle of dismay over the hills of Israel and Judah (cf. Isa 8:21–22). With Galilee converted into the Assyrian province of Megiddo, Shalmaneser V

Conquest of Lachish by the Assyrian army, on a relief from the palace of Sennacherib at Nineveh.

(727–721 B.C.) laid siege to Samaria; the city—and the Northern Kingdom of Israel—fell to his successor, Sargon II (721–705 B.C.) in 721 and was promptly incorporated into the Assyrian provincial system (2 Kgs 17:6).

Egypt, the goal all along, was now in sight, and Assyria was not to be stayed. In 720 B.C. Sargon defeated the Egyptian general Re'u at Raphia south of Gaza, bringing Philistia into the Assyrian fold. He campaigned against Arab tribes in the southern Levant in 716 B.C., then squelched revolts by the kings of Ashdod (egged on by Egypt) in 713 and 712. Yet Sargon had to be careful with Philistia: this was the last bastion of natural and human resources prior to the Sinai road to Egypt, and Assyria's supply lines were already stretched razor thin. Assyrian policy seems to have been to allow key trade cities such as Gaza, Ashkelon and Ashdod to continue to function relatively normally, apparently to support Assyria's final harsh march across the Sinai desert. Or, Assyria hoped that Philistia (and Judah, which also retained semi-independent vassal, rather than provincial, status) could at least be buffer states to absorb potential Egyptian attempts to stop Assyria from entering the Sinai.

Sennacherib (705–681 B.C.) managed to subdue Hezekiah's resistance in Judah (701 B.C.) and also destroy Babylon (689 B.C.), thereby establishing a semblance of *Pax Assyriaca* across the empire and enjoy the hard-won fruit of his labor (a bit of a flourish can be seen in art, literature and building activity during his reign). But the Assyrian empire was reaching the end of its natural limits. In 671 B.C. Sennacherib's son Esarhaddon (680–669 B.C.) finally did get into Lower Egypt (Memphis). His successor, Ashurbanipal (669–627 B.C.), also a kind of Renaissance man, sacked Thebes in Upper Egypt in 663, culminating Assyria's centuries-long goal of world domination. The empire was badly overextended, and Egypt proved too remote to hold. Quickly burning through what was left of its now-aging youthful energy, the "Might that was Assyria"[31] collapsed and within five short decades had fallen to Babylon. Like fireworks, the Assyrian Empire had a long, promising rise followed by a quick burst of brilliance, and then nothing.[32]

*   *   *   *   *

While the Assyrian kings were attempting to orchestrate a series of events that would take them all the way to Egypt by the middle of the first millennium B.C., the kings of Israel and Judah were occupied with local affairs. The time gap between the withdrawal of Egypt's Ramesside Dynasty from the southern Levant at the end of the second millennium and the appearance of Tiglath-pileser III in Galilee in the mid-eighth century B.C. provided a window of opportunity in which several emerging nation states in and around Canaan all competed for the rights to control the regional economy and tap into world markets at the same time. Solomon, Asa, Jehoshaphat,

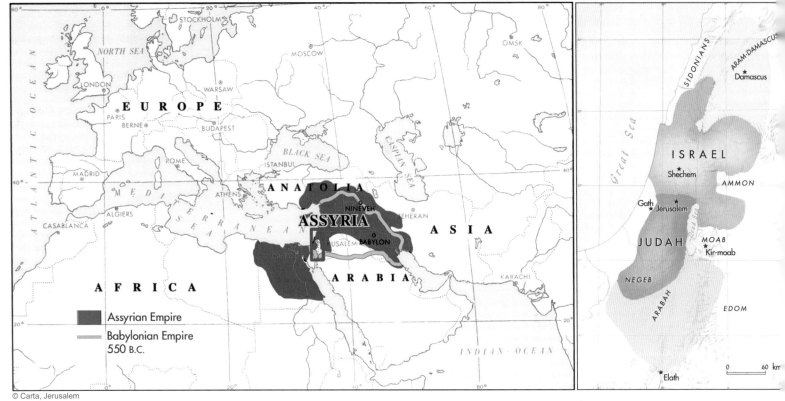

Assyrian Empire
Babylonian Empire
550 B.C.

© Carta, Jerusalem

Ahab, Uzziah and the second Jeroboam were all pretty success-ful. Absent any real threats from large powers outside the region, the struggles for area supremacy that we read about on the pages of the books of Joshua, Judges, Samuel and First Kings, though quite real for their participants, were actually relatively small, and localized within the larger world stage. The individual nation states of the southern Levant (Israel, Judah, Aram-Damascus, Ammon, Moab, Edom, Phoenicia and the Philistine confederation) took turns rising and falling, with their horizons for control (with rare exception) realistically limited to the immediate area. In the spirit of tribalism from which these nations had sprung, coalitions would come together or fall apart, depending on the priorities and felt needs of the moment.

The largest attempt at coalition was, of course, that led by Hadad-ezer of Damascus and Ahab of Israel against Shalmaneser III at Qarqar in 853 B.C. (Jehoshaphat of Judah may have been a participant although he is not named in the sources).[33] Regional differences were set aside to face a larger, common enemy on the Levant's northern frontier. When the Assyrians actually arrived at the borders of Israel a century later, the reality of the situation made attempts at holding together a coalition much more difficult: with the cat at the door, some mice felt it expedient to learn how to purr. In the meantime, Israel's response in 841 B.C. to Shalmaneser III's move against Damascus and the Galilee is evident for all to see on the storied Black Obelisk of Shalmaneser.[34] In the only image that we have of a king of Israel or Judah from the ancient world, Jehu of Israel (841–814 B.C.) kneels prostrate before the Assyrian king, his face nearly touching the ground.

The kingdoms of Israel and Judah enjoyed a local resurgence in the late ninth and early eighth centuries B.C. while Assyria minded to matters closer to home, with Uzziah (767–740 B.C.) and Jeroboam II (782–753 B.C.) positioning themselves to share the wealth of a restored Kingdom of Solomon. But the Assyrians, absent in body though present in mind, were remembered, and the prophet Jonah son of Amitati from Gath-hepher, eager to encourage Jeroboam's

expansion northward (2 Kgs 14:25), was in no mood to help fa-cilitate God's mercy toward Nineveh (the book of Jonah). He was certainly not alone in his sentiment. According to Assyrian sources (the Bible is silent on this one), the good king Uzziah led a coali-tion against Tiglath-pileser III in 743 B.C. but was unsuccessful in stopping the advance.[35] But Uzziah's contemporary, Menahem of Israel (752–742 B.C.) was forced to pay tribute to Assyria, reducing Israel to vassal-state status (2 Kgs 15:19–20).

With Tiglath-pileser III engaged against Urartu in the far north in 735 B.C., Pekah of Israel (740–732 B.C.) and Rezin of Aram-Damascus thought it a good time to restart the coalition of a century before. Ahaz of Judah (735–716 B.C.) refused to join, and the at-tempt to force him to do so led to what has become known as the Syro-Ephraimite War (Isa 7:1–16). Sensing an opportunity in only the first year of his reign, Ahaz asked Tiglath-pileser for help, perhaps hoping that by becoming an Assyrian agent in the southern Levant he could reap local benefits at the expense of his pesky neighbors. A young Isaiah thoroughly condemned Ahaz' expediency—it was the prophet's first foray into the arena of international politics—and spoke of impending "distress, darkness and the gloom of anguish" (Isa 8:22). Sure enough, Rezin's kingdom was taken in 732 B.C., on the last of Tiglath-pileser's three lightning strikes into the southern Levant. Even though Galilee was now "of the Gentiles" (cf. Isa 9:1), Ahaz of Judah remained true to form by introducing pro-Assyrian innovations within the Temple confines of Jerusalem. Because we lack independent evidence to suggest that the Assyrians forced conquered peoples to adopt Assyrian religion, we can assume that Ahaz acted willingly.

With the Galilee and Jezreel Valley, northern Transjordan and the Phoenician coast all converted into formal Assyrian provinces, Hoshea, the last king of Israel (732–721 B.C., waffled in panic: he first managed to keep intact the vassal status of the what was left of the kingdom of Isarel by paying tribute to Shalmaneser V, then, under the urging of So (Osorkon IV) of Egypt, stopped (2 Kgs 17:3–4). The Assyrian siege on Samaria, Israel's capital, was im-

18

mediate (725–721 B.C.)—and effective: Israel was added to the list of Assyrian provinces. Sargon recorded that 27,280 Israelites were taken into permanent exile and replaced with people from other parts of the empire (2 Kgs 17:6, 24)[36]. For its part, Egypt—with a history of being both a friendly ally and a meddlesome outsider in the southern Levant—had its own priorities in egging Hoshea on. As they had managed to do under Rameses II, Egypt wanted a buffer of docile nation states across the Sinai that, as they were being eaten, would satisfy or at least slow down the ravenous Assyrian advance.

Assyria had only Judah and the independent-minded city states of Philistia to bring into line, though Hezekiah (716–687 B.C.) at least had no real intention of going along. Hezekiah broke the vassal status of his father Ahaz (2 Kgs 18:7) and prepared his kingdom for greatness. All available archaeological and textual witnesses about the situation of Judah and Jerusalem in the late eighth century B.C. agree that Hezekiah's efforts at strengthening his kingdom were extensive (e.g. Isa 22:8–11).[37] Sargon II had perished in battle on Assyria's far northern frontier in 705 B.C., and the possibility remained that Sennacherib would not be able to follow up on his father's campaigns in the southern Levant. If he could not, Hezekiah's Judah would reign supreme; if he did, Hezekiah would be ready for war against a relatively inexperienced Assyrian king campaigning far from home. Scholars remain divided on whether Sennacherib campaigned against Judah once (701 B.C.) or twice (the second time perhaps in 688 B.C.) and exactly when in the struggle Egypt intervened under Taharqa (2 Kgs 19:9). All agree, though, on the result: Judah was totally devastated and Hezekiah's kingdom reduced to what lay within the walls of Jerusalem, "like a bird in a cage"[38] (2 Kgs 18:13–19:36). Though severely clipped, Judah retained its vassal status, thereby avoiding the ultimate national indignity of its northern neighbors, and preserving the possibility to enjoy (though not for several decades) the chance to live again.

Sennacherib's attack on Judah is the only event that is told in the Hebrew Bible three times (2 Kgs 18–19; 2 Chron 32; Isa 37). It wasn't Judah's finest hour, but it was, so to speak, one of God's. Writing prophecy began in Israel under the response of the Israelite and Judean kings to the hammer blows of Assyria (e.g. Isa 5:26-30; 10:5-11, 24-32; 20:4; and the "scorched-earth" march of Isa

37:24-27), and Isaiah, Micah and Hosea had plenty to say about the reaction of their national leadership to events on the ground. Hosea's head-shaking assessment is typical:

Ephraim is a silly, senseless pigeon—
  Now calling upon Egypt, now turning to Assyria for help.
                                         (Hos 7:11; cf. 9:3; 10:5–6)

But the heart of the message was much more personal. The overall prophetic attitude held that Assyria was in the process of defeating Israel and Judah not because Asshur was a superior deity or that the Assyrian god commanded a superior army, but because the LORD God of Israel willed it as punishment for sin. Personal, social, economic and national injustices had grown too heavy, the prophet inveighed, and Assyria was God's handy instrument for correcting what needed correcting (e.g. Isa 7:18–19; 10:5–6). Isaiah in particular stood out against foreign alliances of any kind, since the LORD God was sufficient to look after the affairs of his own nation. Isaiah's prophetic ministry spanned the decades of the direct Assyrian encounter with Israel and Judah; a young prophet during the advent of very difficult times, his convictions became more firm with age. God would be true to His covenantal promises, and his kings (such as Ahaz!) should remain faithful as well (cf. Isa 7:9). Jerusalem, God had ordained, would be spared "for My own sake and for the sake of My servant David" (Isa 37:35), certainly not because of any competency or preparedness of Hezekiah (cf. Isa 22:1–11). Isaiah longed for a day when a son of David would be worthy of the titles "Wonderful Counselor, Mighty God, Eternal Father, Prince of Peace" (Isa 9:6; cf. Isa 40–66).

Isaiah's vision for Israel's future was, in a sense, the last word on Assyria. The prophet Nahum, however, snuck in some political poetic justice. Writing sometime in the interval between Assyria's climactic defeat of Thebes (No-Amon, "The City of Amun"; Nahum 3:8) in 663 B.C. and their utter collapse to Babylon five decades later, Nahum's imagery overflowed with the blood and guts, eye-for-eye vengeance of God:

Woe to the bloody city,
  completely full of lies and pillage . . .
Are there any on whom your ceaseless cruelty has not born down?
                                         (Nahum 3:1, 19)

Today's grain fields stretch beyond remains of an Israelite storehouse at Hazor, covering the expanse of what once had been the large Canaanite city of the Middle and Late Bronze Ages. Isaiah commented on the brief history of the empires of his world: "Scarcely have they been planted, scarcely have they been sown, scarcely has their stock taken root in the earth, but He merely blows on them and they wither" (Isa 40:24).

The Neo-Babylonian Empire and Judah's Last Hurrah

When the Assyrian Empire collapsed into a pile of rubble in the late seventh century B.C. it left no lasting legacy. For the ancient Greeks, whose historians and geographers sought to preserve a record of the peoples of the ancient Near East for the reading audience of the emerging Mediterranean world, Assyria was already a distant memory. Not so Babylon. Even though the lifespan of the Babylonian Empire was a scant 87 years (626–539 B.C.), its heritage was remembered in the classical world and has endured until today. This was in part due to of the special status already accorded Babylon in its own day, as the world center of religion, culture, science, literature and the arts. Indeed, the Neo-Babylonian Period is the second-best attested period of ancient Mesopotamia in number of surviving cuneiform sources, following only the Sumerian renaissance of Ur III (c. 2100–2000 B.C.). Babylon's status as the urban repository for what was truly Mesopotamian—like Athens was to Greece—gave it a legacy for cultural greatness that was revered by even its political enemies. The Neo-Babylonian kings exploited this reputation as they fostered what can only be described as an intentional interest in their own past (Nabonidus, the empire's last monarch, even sponsored an archaeological excavation of the *E-Gipar* temple in Ur). But even more so, the legacy of the short-lived Neo-Babylonian Empire endures today because it was Nebuchadnezzar who conquered Jerusalem, destroyed the Temple and took a large number of influential and capable Judeans back to "the waters of Babylon" (Ps 137:1)—and it was these Jews who, in spite of adverse circumstances, created a live and vibrant community in exile that existed well into the twentieth century A.D.

This is not to say that Babylon didn't have its nasty side. Indeed, their military machinery was as bloody as that of the Assyrians against whom they had struggled for centuries. The Assyria-Babylon fight for political control of Mesopotamia was unrelenting, with the centuries of Assyrian ascendancy (c. 1200–700 B.C.) witnessing one frustrated attempt by Babylon for self-rule after another.[39] The Assyrian kings Sennacherib and Esarhaddon both placed their own sons as vassal kings over Babylon, as their efforts at empire-building focused on a push to Egypt in the first half of the seventh century B.C. Continuing the policy of family rule, Ashurbanipal of Assyria (669–627 B.C.) made his brother Shamash-shum-ukin king of Babylon in 667 B.C. Yet Babylon was slowly able to gain economic (and political) strength anyway. Twenty years later, as Assyria was in the early throes of collapse, brother turned on brother as Babylon challenged the Assyrian throne. Civil war raged in Babylon for four years (652–648 B.C.), with Tyre, various west Arabian states and probably Judah backing Babylon. Shamash-shum-ukin perished in the flames of his own palace in 648 B.C., and Ashurbanipal called in the heads of all of the western states, including Judah's Manasseh, for renewed pledges of loyalty. Needing a loyal ally on his southwestern frontier, Ashurbanipal allowed Manasseh room to reassert himself (2 Chron 33:11-17). Much to Ashurbanipal's chagrin, Babylon would soon take the same liberty at independence.

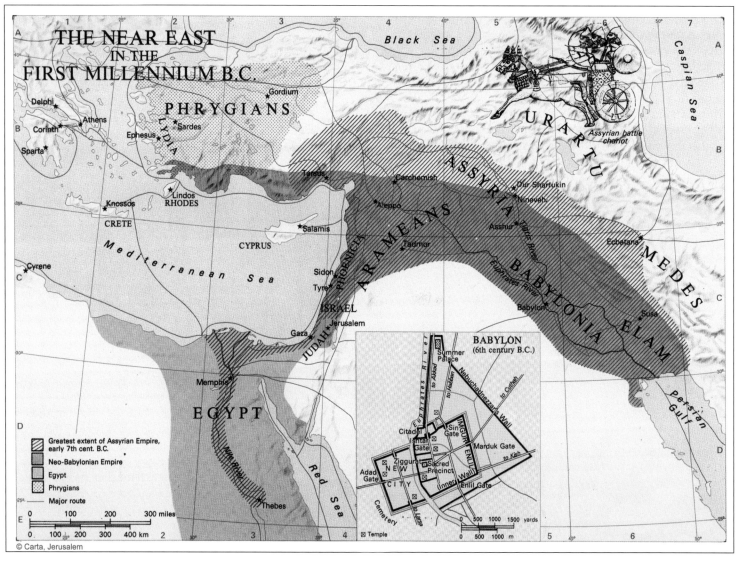

When Ashurbanipal died in 627 B.C. Babylon finally had its day, and was able to achieve real independence for the first and only time since the days of Hammurapi.[40] Indeed, the Neo-Babylonian Empire was the last native dynasty to rule Mesopotamia. The catalyst was Nabopolassar (625–605 B.C.), Chaldean governor of "Sealand," the swampy, southernmost region of Mesopotamia where the Tigris and Euphrates Rivers dump into the Persian Gulf. "Chaldean" is an ethnic term, designating people belonging to a confederation of West-Semitic speaking tribes that populated this rural swamp land and controlled the lucrative trade routes coming out of the Gulf. Politically the Chaldeans were fiercely anti-Assyrian and ended up taking control of large urban centers such as Babylon and Uruk, from which they could begin to unify their emerging pan-Babylonian empire.

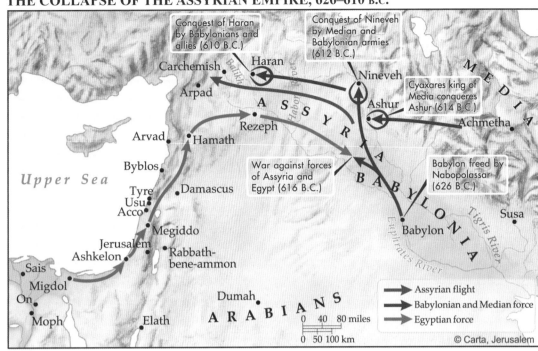

THE COLLAPSE OF THE ASSYRIAN EMPIRE, 626–610 B.C.

The Chaldeans must have been related to the Arameans, another indigenous people from southern Mesopotamia that is mentioned in the cuneiform sources, which likewise fought for Babylonian independence from Assyria.

These native Babylon forces coalesced around Nabopolassar, who took firm charge of the city of Babylon by 623 B.C. With the Medes (from the mountainous northern Persian plateau), Nabopolassar defeated a coalition of Assyrian and Egyptian forces out west in 616 (sensing a new power rising in the East, Assyria and Egypt actually joined forces in what would lead to the death throes of Assyria and the political irrelevance of Egypt). Nebopolassar forged a formal treaty with the Medes in 614 B.C., sealing it by marrying his son, Nebuchadnezzar,[41] to the Median mountain princess Amytis (it was to please her that Nebuchadnezzar would one day build the celebrated Hanging Gardens in Babylon[42]). From here the battle sequence was rapid and chillingly effective: Cyaxares the Mede captured Asshur in 614 B.C.; he and Nabopolassar seized the Assyrian capital Nineveh two years later; and in 610 the last viable bits of the Assyrian state were smothered at Haran. An Egyptian force under Neco II tried, and failed, to prop up the last Assyrian king, Ashur-uballit II, by attempting to retake Haran in 609 (Judah's Josiah lost his life in the process; 2 Kgs 23:29; 2 Chron 35:20–24). Nabopolassar elevated his crown prince Nebuchadnezzar to co-regent in 607, and it was he who engineered the final Assyrian defeat at Carchemish in 605 B.C. (although the battle was really against a resurgent Egypt that was bent on taking control of the Levant for the first time since the height of the Rameside Period six centuries prior; cf. Jer 46:2). In any case, the Babylonians emerged as clear victors, and a young and energetic Nebuchadnezzar (604–562 B.C.) pushed southward into the Levant, as far as Hamath on the mid-Orontes.

With Assyria gone, the only two serious contenders for world domination other than Babylon were the Medes (who were friendly) and Egypt, who had just been pushed down the Levantine throat. Nebuchadnezzar quickly followed up with a series of almost yearly campaigns against Hatti-land (Syria and Palestine). The first thrust was deep, all the way to Ashkelon, in the first year of his sole reign (604 B.C.); this is the only city in the region preserved by name in the

Babylonian Chronicles. Judah, under its squirming king Jehoiakim, promptly became a Babylonian vassal (2 Kgs 24:1). Campaigns to Philistia in 603 and 602 B.C. managed to turn the southern coastal plain into a Babylonian launch-pad facing the Sinai, but the next year Nebuchadnezzar met his match against Egypt at Gaza, the old pharonic doorway into Asia (Jer 47:1). Emboldened, Jehoiakim ceased paying tribute to Nebuchadnezzar (2 Kgs 24:1).

Nebuchadnezzar never would make it to the land of the Pharaohs, but at least he contained Egypt to within its historic Nile Valley borders. Taking the next year to regroup, the Babylonian king returned to the southern Levant with a vengeance, with the goal of at least subduing everything up to the eastern edge of the Sinai and enjoying the full economic privileges of this land between. He conquered various Arabian tribes in 599, then, after a two-year campaign (598–597 B.C.), forced Judah back into the Babylonian fold (2 Kgs 24:10–16). Further campaigns in the Levant in 596, 594 and 593 B.C. set the table for Nebuchadnezzar's gorged feast

The god Marduk on a piece of lapis lazuli, from Babylon. "You, Marduk, are the most honored of the great gods, your decree is unrivaled, [even over] the sky-god. From this day onward your pronouncements shall be unchangeable, to raise up or bring low—those shall be in your hand" (Enuma Elish [the Babylonian Genesis] IV, 5–8).

THE CLOSING YEARS OF THE KINGDOM OF JUDAH

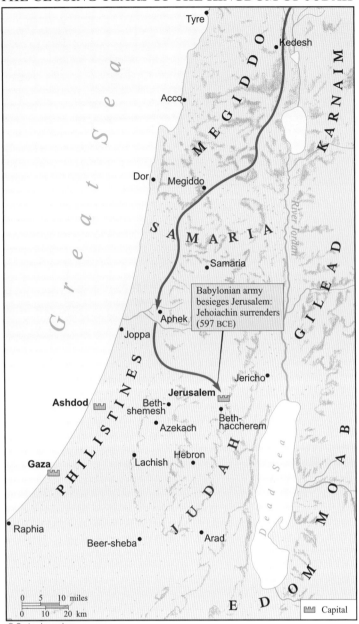

Babylonian army besieges Jerusalem: Jehoiachin surrenders (597 BCE)

© Carta, Jerusalem

reflected the Babylonian conviction that *this* was the connection point between god and man. Everything touched by Nebuchadnezzar heighted the "Greatness that was Babylon."[45]

But it was not to last. Like Assyria, the empire of Babylon fell suddenly, but this time, with internal subterfuge. Succeeded by his son Amel-Marduk (Evil-merodach; 561–560 B.C.), then son-in-law Neriglissar (559–556 B.C.) and finally grandson Labashi-Marduk (three months of 556 B.C.), Nebuchadnezzar's dynastic line was snipped by Nabonidus (555–539 B.C.), an elderly Aramean usurper from Haran who seemed to be more interested in matters of personal introspection than affairs of state. Nabonidus spent ten of his sixteen years on the throne in self-imposed exile at the Arabian oasis of Teima, a center, like Haran and Ur (both home cities of Abraham), of the moon-god Sîn. He left his son Belshazzar in charge back in Babylon (cf. Dan 5:1). When Nabonidus returned to Babylon in 540 (or 542) B.C., he handed the wealthy Marduk temples over to the priests of Sîn. The powerful Marduk priesthood responded by opening the city to Cyrus II and the Persians on October 12, 539 B.C.[46]

* * * * *

The kingdom of Judah entered the seventh century B.C. on life-support. Hezekiah, reigning over a much reduced kingdom in the wake of Sennacherib's attack and no doubt chafing at what could have been, died a beaten vassal in 686 B.C. His son Manasseh succeeded him, and although Manasseh received the stamp of disapproval by the writers of Kings and Chronicles for not continuing the Temple-based reform policies of his dutiful father, his lengthy reign (at 55 years it was the longest of any king of Israel or Judah) coincided with the beginning of Assyria's collapse and so gave Judah enough stability to strengthen and recover (cf. 2 Kgs 21:1–18; 2 Chron 33:1–20). By the time the capable Josiah took the throne in 640 B.C., Assyria had fallen back behind the Euphrates, but Babylon was on the rise. So was Judah, on the pattern of a young Hezekiah, or even Solomon.

Josiah expanded his borders to include Judean and Israelite

THE FINAL CAMPAIGN OF NEBUCHADNEZZAR AGAINST JUDAH

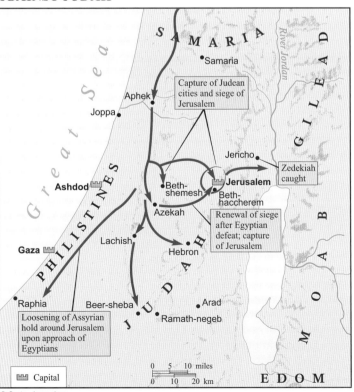

Capture of Judean cities and siege of Jerusalem

Zedekiah caught

Renewal of siege after Egyptian defeat; capture of Jerusalem

Loosening of Assyrian hold around Jerusalem upon approach of Egyptians

© Carta, Jerusalem

of 587–586 B.C., in which Jerusalem was destroyed and the kingdom of Judah ceased to exist (2 Kgs 25:1–21; 2 Chron 36:11–20; Jer 39:1–10).[43] For Nebuchadnezzar, it was simple expediency to secure his extreme southwestern frontier. Taking a page out of the Assyrian playbook, Nebuchadnezzar took the best and brightest of the Judeans to Babylon (in 597, 586 and 582 B.C.; 2 Kgs 24:15–16; 25:11–21), although unlike his Assyrian predecessors he allowed these captives to live in their own colonies and did not repopulate Judah with foreigners from other captured lands.

The 43-year reign of Nebuchadnezzar defined the entire Neo-Babylonian Period. His early military success bent the channels of economic wealth from Assyria to Babylon, allowing the king to expend considerable energy rebuilding cities and temples back home. It was the capital city Babylon, place of ancient wonder and awe, that benefited the most. Nebuchadnezzar even attached a museum to his royal palace where he could display statues, stela and other inscribed relics of Mesopotamia's glorious past. The classic Mesopotamian creation epic, *Enuma Elish*, gained prominence as it justified the rise of the city of Babylon to the top of the political heap down on earth and its god, Marduk, to the head of the pantheon in heaven.[44] Marduk's main temple in Babylon, *E-temen-an-ki*, "the House of the Foundation of Heaven and Earth," bore a name that territory that the Assyrians had converted into provinces, from Philistia to Galilee and Transjordan. At the same time, he centered the kingdom's political, economic and especially religious life on Jerusalem (2 Kgs 22:1–23:27; 2 Chron 34:1–8; 35:1). In pattern, this was similar to what the last kings of Assyria had done with Nineveh, or Nebuchadnezzar at Babylon. Josiah's efforts were Judah's last—and perhaps greatest—hurrah, but they ended in sudden tragedy. In 609 B.C. Josiah lost his life in his prime, cut down in an attempt to meet and defeat Egypt's newly enthroned Pharaoh Neco II as the latter was driving the Egyptian army up Josiah's coast to Carchemish (2 Kgs 23:29–30; 2 Chron 35:20–25).

Independence had lasted less than two decades before Judah was again caught in a tightening vise, this time between the jaws of Egypt and Babylon. Even though Neco II failed in his attempt to stop Babylon at Haran (609 B.C.), he was able to hold on to the Levant and replaced Josiah's successor Jehoahaz with his quiescent older brother, Jehoiakim (2 Kgs 23:30–34). The new Judean king did the only thing that was politically prudent to do: for four years he played the role of a loyal Egyptian vassal, then switched sides after Nebuchadnezzar pushed to Ashkelon and drove the Egyptians back into the Sinai (2 Kgs 23:35; 24:1). But when Neco countered by checking Nebuchadnezzar at Gaza (601 B.C.), temporarily removing Babylonian pressure, Jehoiakim withheld tribute. Like Hezekiah, he risked the life of his kingdom by calculating that the Empire wouldn't strike back (2 Kgs 24:1).

The die was now firmly cast. The failed invasion of Sennacherib a century before showed that God would protect his own people, but the lesson taken was that God would do so no matter what, with the "no matter what" being that personal and national behavior didn't matter much since God wouldn't (or couldn't) let his kingdom fall. This fatal flaw in moral logic, breaking the nexus between behavior and consequence, was announced by the prophets Jeremiah and Habakkuk and corrected by God's unwitting but very willing agent, the Babylonians (Jer 5:14–17; Hab 1:5–11). The old tribal religious center of Shiloh had fallen, Jeremiah reminded both people and king; Jerusalem would as well (Jer 7:12–15; 26:1–6). It was better, the prophet counseled, to submit to Babylon and await God's favor (Jer 27:1–22). Judah would be destroyed, not because Nebuchadnezzar and his god Marduk were all-powerful, but because the LORD God willed it as punishment for Judah's sins (Jer 5:1–13). It was not a popular message: Jeremiah was imprisoned repeatedly (Jer 20:1–6; 32:1–5; 37:11–16; 38:1–13), threatened with death (Jer 26:7–11), and his written words burned (Jer 36:1–26) by a ruling class that preferred to court the help of Egypt as the means of restoring a semblance of Josiah's now-gone kingdom. Realistically, it was all a recipe for disaster.

Whether at Babylon's urging or, like Judah, in hope of expanding their own kingdoms in Nebuchadnezzar's short absence, bands of Arameans, Ammonites and Moabites, with Chaldeans(!) pushed into Judah's soft eastern underbelly (2 Kgs 24:2). The Judean king died in December 598, and his young and inexperienced son Je-

THE EXILE FROM JUDAH AND THE FLIGHT TO EGYPT

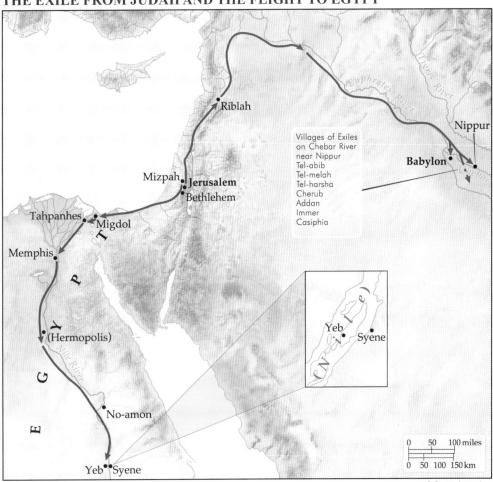

© Carta, Jerusalem

hoiachin was unable to keep Nebuchadnezzar out of Jerusalem the following year (March, 597 B.C.). Jehoiachin was exiled to Babylon and his uncle, Zedekiah, installed as vassal (2 Kgs 24:8–20). For Judah the next decade was one of political chaos, failed diplomatic missions (cf. Jer 27:3), territorial encroachments especially by the Edomites,[47] and renewed egging from Egypt to revolt (as always, Egypt was eager for Judah to be a diversion whenever their own nation was threatened from the north). The result was as tragic as it was certain: the cities and countryside of Judah were devastated and this time Jerusalem too was destroyed (19 July, 586 B.C.; 2 Kgs 25:1–21).

Many Judeans, including the royal family, were exiled to Babylon; others fled the opposite way, to Egypt (Jeremiah was taken to Tahpanes in the northeastern Delta by his own people and against his will; Jer 43:1–8; 44:1; cf. Jer 46:13–14). Nebuchadnezzar governed what was left of Judah through Gedaliah, a Judean appointee who was promptly assassinated by partisans in Mizpah (2 Kgs 25:22–26; Jer 40:7–41:3). Although archaeological evidence (especially at Ketef Hinnom outside of Jerusalem) suggests that Judah was not left destitute, the life of the kingdom was over, the Temple was burned to the ground and many of the people had scattered. Yet God's prophets offered hope:

The LORD's lovingkindnesses indeed never cease,
  for His compassions never fail.
They are new every morning;
  great is Your faithfulness.
"The LORD is my portion," says my soul,
  "Therefore I have hope in Him."

Lamentations 3:22–24

And in Judah, Babylon and Egypt, the remnant began to grow.

The Persian Empire and the Return from Exile

The Persian Empire was a bridge carrying the world of the ancient Near East into the Mediterranean. By penetrating the Fertile Crescent from the mountainous Iranian plateau, then pushing out the other side to Libya and the Aegean, the Persian kings opened new gateways into and out of the periphery that surrounded the old, comfortable river valleys of Mesopotamia and Egypt. In doing so, they would set the stage for the pendulum of the ancient world to make a dramatic swing—though not eastward to Persia, but west to Greece.

The Persian Empire rose in the wake of a kind of expedient cooperation between the Medes and the Babylonians, each of whom shared the goal of supplanting the Assyrian Empire. The Persians were related to the Medes; both were Aryan populations that had entered Iran from the rugged mountains to the north and west and settled its high plateau sometime before the beginning of the first millennium B.C. The Medes made their home between the Zagros Mountains and the Caspian Sea, northeast of Assyria, while the Persians filled the plateau farther south, opposite Babylon. The Medes reached their height under Cyaxares (625–585 B.C.), who, with a rising Babylon, managed to chase the vestiges of the Assyrian Empire into the sunset, across the top of the Fertile Crescent from Asshur to Nineveh to Haran (in 614, 612 and 610 B.C. respectively). By the time he died, Cyaxares had taken the Medes deep into western Anatolia. In forging a peace treaty with the Lydians, Cyaxares formalized an Indo-European link between Europe and Asia that would only grow stronger in the centuries ahead, first under Persian, then Greek and Roman control.

But Median dominance was short-lived. Within four decades Cyrus the Persian (also known as Cyrus II; 550–530 B.C.) consolidated his control over the most powerful of the Persian tribes, then, with the backing of the Babylonian monarch Nabonidus, revolted against his grandfather Astyages, the Median overlord. The Median army defected to Cyrus, making him heir to a ready-made empire. Cyrus validated his control by a quick thrust to Lydia, where in 547 B.C. he defeated Croesus at Sardis, 45 miles from the Aegean Sea. The years 546-540 B.C. were likely spent consolidating Persia's rugged eastern frontier. This left Babylon, which Cyrus (now "the

Great") took without battle in October 539 B.C. Thus was founded the Persian (or, Achaemenid) Empire: the hordes from the periphery had conquered the cultured center.

Cyrus' public voice chose to attribute his success in taking Babylon to the permissive will of the Babylonian national god Marduk, who was punishing Nabonidus for opposing his divine will (and that of his powerful priests) in internal matters related to Nabonidus' elevation of the moon god Sîn. Be that as it may, Cyrus' public assessment also reflects an attitude—certainly permissive by ancient standards—which tolerated local religious and nationalistic feelings. Specifically, in the decree recorded in the so-called Cyrus Cylinder, Cyrus reiterated his peaceful and friendly intentions in taking over Babylon. In doing so, he also reaffirmed the *kidinnūtu* (privileged) status long held by the city and its temples, ordered the return of cult statues exiled by Nabonidus back to their own temples across the Tigris.[48] By favoring local temples generally and not just those of Babylon, Cyrus was able to acknowledge the historic role of the greatest of the old Mesopotamian cities while decentralizing its importance in the new world order. Through such diplomacy, Cyrus apparently sought to foster compliance of far-flung populations to Persian control and will (it was a policy that appreciated the carrot as much as the stick).

Cyrus' son and successor Cambyses (530–522 B.C.) conquered Egypt with the help of an Arabian king in 525 B.C.. That act verified the need to cultivate friendly forces deep in the southern Levant. His successor was Darius I (522–486 B.C.), who hailed from a collateral Achaemenid line. Darius had to retake Egypt in 519 B.C. as part of a show of force putting down revolts across the empire (including two by pretenders to the Babylonian throne, Nebuchadnezzar III and Nebuchadnezzar IV, in 522 and 521 B.C.). But Darius' main direction of conquest was, like Cyaxares, northwest toward Greece. With the help of the Phoenician navy Darius conquered Thrace in 513 B.C., then, after subduing various Hellenic cities in and around Ionia (498–493 B.C.), established control over Macedonia (492 B.C.). For a brief moment (until the Persian defeat at Marathon two years later), the farthest extent of the Persian Empire reached from the Indus River to Greece and Libya (Alexander's empire would scarcely be larger). The borders formed a massive rectangle of sea and land, encompassing the maximal size of the Egyptian, Assyrian and Babylonian empires together with hundreds of miles of "wild frontier"—now the new center—lying beyond.

As with Rameses II for the New Kingdom of Egypt or Nebuchadnezzar for Babylon, Darius I represents in both reality and public imagination the golden age of ancient Persia. Darius organized what was otherwise an unwieldy empire into twenty semi-autonomous districts called satrapies.[49] Egypt was one; *eber nāri*, "Beyond the River," was another, encompassing everything from the Euphrates River to the border of Egypt, essentially the territory once under Solomon's rule (cf. 1 Kgs 4:21, 24).[50] Esther 1:1 mentions 127 Persian provinces, which must indicate a total of the inner divisions within the satrapies; in Beyond the River, these included Yehud, Idumea, Ashdod, Sidon, Samaria, Galilee, Karnaim, Gilead, Ammon and Moab. The

THE SATRAPIES OF THE PERSIAN EMPIRE

Persian Empire
SEISTAN Persian satrapy
Royal road

0   300   600 miles
0   400   800 km

© Carta, Jerusalem

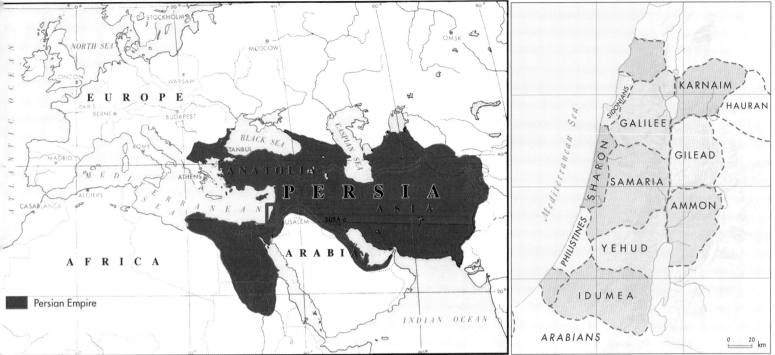

Carta, Jerusalem

ethnic groups populating each province were allowed a degree of cultural freedom as long as they paid their taxes on time.

Administratively, Darius standardized a system of weights and measures, was the first monarch of the ancient world to make wide use of coinage, appointed a system of courts and judges, organized an official postal system that ran the Royal Road (by which a traveler could cover the 1700 miles from Susa to Sardis in 90 days), and dug a canal connecting the Nile with the Gulf of Suez. As for his capital cities, Darius passed over Ectabana, the old Median administrative center, and Pasargadae, capital of Cyrus (both were too remote), as well as Babylon, which was too open, for Susa on the east Babylonian plain (his administrative center) and Persepolis, a majestic high plateau retreat. The over-the-top description of the royal banquets at Susa, hosted by Ahasuerus (Xerxes; 486–464 B.C.) in the days of Esther the Queen, at which even the horses wore crowns (Esther 1:1–9; cf. 6:7–9), says enough.

Yet all was never well. What the Persian Empire lacked was a cohesive feeling of nationalism and a firm internal authority to compel unity over its disparate parts. So even at its height under Darius I, the viability of Persian Empire was squeezed. The most obvious pressure point was in the Aegean, the direction of Persia's most determined advance. Darius' defeat at Marathon in 490 B.C. merely anticipated a greater route by the Greeks of Persian forces under Xerxes at the bay of Salamis off Athens in 479 B.C. The Aegean was never again Persian, giving Greece rise to their Classic Age. A second pressure point was Egypt. In spite of the well-trod path of empires through the Levant and the support for Persia by a Phoenician fleet that ruled what was once an Egyptian east Mediterranean sea, the Egyptians had too deep a history of independence to submit easily to foreign control. Egypt revolted against Persia three times: in 484–483 B.C., with the help of Athens in 463–454 B.C., and again from 404 B.C. through the middle of the next century. Ezra's return to Jerusalem with financial and tax concessions from the Persian treasury coincided with the second Egyptian revolt, and with it one might suppose that Yehud, a province in the southern Levant facing Egypt, was strengthened to aid Persian efforts at holding the line.

The third pressure point was from within: the persistent tendency toward revolt in the satrapies and provinces. One of the more important revolts for its possible repercussions in the land of ancient Israel was that led by Megabyzus, the powerful general and brother-in-law of Artaxerxes I (464–424 B.C.) who governed Beyond the River. Megabyzus' revolt, which took place sometime after 454 B.C., was suppressed shortly before Nehemiah's state-sanctioned mission to rebuild the fortress and walls of Jerusalem (Neh 2:8). The Persians built "fortresses" and "walls" to house military garrisons which would serve not only wartime needs but also control and tax the local population (note that officers and cavalry accompanied Nehemiah to Jerusalem; Neh 2:9) The leaders of Samaria (Sanballat), Ammon (Tobiah) and Arabia (Geshem), provinces surrounding Yehud, naturally opposed Nehemiah, but one can imagine that the Persian government as well likely wanted to temper local ambitions that could lead to further unrest. All this suggests that it was in Artaxerxes' interest to dispatch Nehemiah to Yehud in order to ensure a loyal and compliant ally on his vulnerable southwestern frontier. With the main focus of Persian attention on the Susa-to-Sardis corridor in the north, Artaxerxes needed a quiet(er) border facing Egypt.

But in the end, a continuous series of uprisings throughout the western provinces, many instigated by Egypt (a familiar role played by the pharaohs against other would-be Asian empires in the past), sufficiently weakened the western defenses of the Persian Empire so that Alexander, who started his own march in 334 B.C., could easily push on through.

*   *   *   *   *

The biblical writers believed that the Persian kings Cyrus II and Darius I were God's special instruments sent to establish and protect the rights of the Jews in their ancestral homeland (2 Chron 36:22–23; Ezra 1:1–4; 6:1–15). Isaiah even called Cyrus "[God's] shepherd . . . [who] will perform all [His] desires" and "[the LORD's] anointed one whom [He] has taken by the right hand" (Isa 44:28; 45:1). Yet the historical record also shows that, given the practicality of the waters and fertile fields of Babylon (cf. Ps 137:1), many

hemiah, cupbearer to the king (Neh 1:11), was as a Jew an exception in high society.

Yet in spite of the real possibilities of success in Babylon, the rocky hills of Judah (now the Persian province of Yehud) that the Jews had known only through the stories of their ancestors proved to be the locus of a stronger call. Ezekiel's visions of a Temple and people restored, the tribes filling the land from the River of Egypt to Hamath (Ezek 36–37; 40–48), helped to instill the vision for a return home. The decree issued by Cyrus which authorized the Jews to return to Jerusalem with their holy vessels and rebuild the Temple (2 Chron 36:22–23; Ezra 1:1–4), is consistent in tone and intent with the decree of the Cyrus Cylinder, and started the formal process that ended the exile.

Jews simply preferred to stay put. Initially, the Judeans who had been taken into exile were not intentionally assimilated into the economic and social structures of Babylonian life but placed in their own settlements, most within the Nippur region near the Chebar (Kabari) canal (Ezek 1:1–3; 3:15). Yet these settlers were, according to the account of 2 Kings 24:14, among the more capable men of Judah, and one might expect that many learned how to make due in their new home. This including learning Aramaic, which was fast becoming the language and script of everyday activities across the Semitic-speaking world (cf. Dan 2:4), and by it many eventually prospered.

We can trace the vitality of Jewish life in Babylon through the appearance of personal names (primarily those with -*yhw* suffixes) in the cuneiform and Aramaic sources. By the second generation (the mid-sixth century B.C.) children of exiled Judeans were taking Babylonian personal names (note Sheshbazzar, "O Sîn, protect the father" and Zerubbabel, "seed of Babylon"; Ezra 1:8; 3:2), though this likely represented simple expediency rather than a crisis of faith. But by the fourth or fifth generation—the time of Ezra and Nehemiah—Jews were starting to take Jewish names again. The largest corpus of information comes from the cuneiform Murashu texts, dating to the second half of the fifth century B.C.[51] Murashu and his sons were wealthy bankers, and in the texts recording their transactions it is possible to identify about seventy Jewish names (these comprise just three percent of the total). Most Babylonian Jews of the time were engaged in agriculture as sub-lessors of fields or livestock, but eleven (a tiny number) held official positions. Ne-

For the returning Judeans (based on the sources, it is only now proper to call them Jews), the first step was to regain rights in their ancestral homeland by creating a Temple community focused on Jerusalem, even though it be under the political control of Persia. The year after Cyrus' edict a number of Jews returned to Jerusalem with Sheshbazzar, a member of the defunct royal line of David, who was given the titles "prince of Judah" and "governor" (but certainly not "king"; Ezra 1:8; 5:14). Zerubbabel soon followed with others (Ezra 2:1–2). Everyone traced the same bend of the Fertile Crescent that Abraham had trekked over a millennium before; then, once home, Zerubbabel and Jeshua the high priest, like their patriarch, built an altar to God, though on the model of the instructions of Moses (Ezra 3:1–3). In the second year of his return Zerubbabel began to rebuild the Temple, importing cedar wood from Lebanon as had David and Solomon for its first construction (Ezra 3:7). So the foundations for both Temple and peoplehood were put in place. Opposition soon followed from a number of quarters: the generic term was "enemies of Judah and Benjamin" (Ezra 4:1) and likely included remnants of populations that had been moved into the area by the Assyrians over one hundred years before, as well as indigenous neighboring peoples who took advantage of the destabilization caused the Babylonian conquest, and likely even some Judeans who had remained behind during the exile—these were all "old timers" for whom the returnees posed any number of threats. Work on the Temple stalled for several years, but prompted by the prophets Haggai and Zechariah and strengthened by Darius I's

Darius I seated on his throne with crown prince Xerxes behind him, from Persepolis.

THE RETURN FROM EXILE

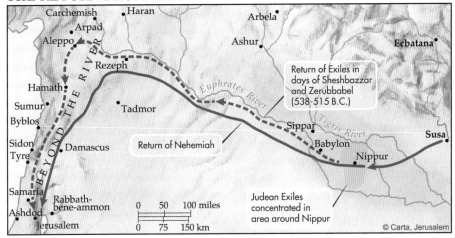

was, after all, a land with natural and persistent geographical divisions that fostered independent living spaces and a constant succession of ambitious men trying to establish control over the scant water and soil resources of the region. Those most upset with Nehemiah's plans to rebuild the walls of Jerusalem were those with the most to lose: Sanballat the Samaritan, Tobiah and Ammonite and Geshem the Arab, each governor of a Persian province bordering Yehud whose people had fought Judah for territorial and economic control of the region for centuries. When Judah was weakened by the Babylonian Exile each gladly had tried to establish their rights to the leftovers. The last thing that Sanballat, Tobiah and Geshem wanted was for a strong Jerusalem to reclaim its historic place in the mix, or for Persia's control in the region to be channeled through the leaders of Yehud. But with his charisma and connections Nehemiah was exactly the kind of leader the community of Jerusalem needed, and work on the walls of Jerusalem was completed within fifty-two days (Neh 6:15).

The end result was a functioning, semi-autonomous province of the Persian Empire, with a lively Jewish identity centered on a Temple rebuilt on holy ground in Jerusalem and a cultural life shaped by the authority of priests and Levites. Political independence was gone, but armed with a realistic working relationship with Persia the Jews of Yehud were able to settle into living patterns that gave them a sense of presence and propriety within the region. It was a formula that worked, and set the tone for what options might be available when a truly foreign power, the Greeks, would arrive on the south Levantine shore toward the end of the fourth century B.C.

renewal of Cyrus' edict, the building was finished and dedicated in 515 B.C. (Ezra 5:1–6:22). Rather than chafe under foreign political control, effective leaders among the Jewish returnees worked within the parameters of the Persian imperial system in order to create as many of the structures of Temple identity that they could. The Jews of Jerusalem and Yehud had an address again.

The next step was to bring the hearts of the people around. The province of Yehud covered the area from Gezer to En-gedi, and Bethel to Beth-zur (surprisingly Hebron was excluded), and many Jews lived outside, in the provinces of Idumea, Ashdod, Sidon (the Sharon Plain) and likely even Samaria. Lacking the cohesion of a Jewish state, boundaries marking their distinctiveness as a people had to be defined. Enter Ezra, a priest and "scribe skilled in the law of Moses" who in 458 B.C. made the journey from Babylon to Jerusalem "to study the Torah of the LORD and to practice it and to teach His statutes and ordinances in Israel" (Ezra 7:1–10). Artaxerxes provided funding and tax concessions for the effort (Ezra 7:6, 11–24), and we would be remiss to think that the Persian king was acting out of altruistic motives. While Ezra used the opportunity to create religious and social structures that attempted to define Jewish distinctiveness in terms of religious behavior consistent with the Law of Moses (Ezra 9:1–10:44), he also followed through on the full decree of the Persian monarch "to appoint magistrates and judges" to judge, teach and enforce "the law of your God and the law of the king" (Ezra 7:25–26). Here the word "law" was not *torah*, but *dat*, a term borrowed from the Persian language meaning "decree" or "royal command" punishable by death, banishment, imprisonment or confiscation of goods. So, given the reality of the times, Ezra was a kind of double-agent: recreating a Torah-observant community in the Jews' ancestral homeland on the one hand, while enforcing a legal environment in the Persian province of Yehud under which local legal traditions could operate within the framework of Persian legal statues on the other. His fight was not against Persia, but people groups in and around Yehud that challenged the divine and empire-mandated Jewish right of return.

The final step was brick and mortar. In 445 B.C. Artaxerxes gave Nehemiah the title "governor of Yehud" and sent him to Jerusalem with the official commission of rebuilding the fortress and walls of Jerusalem. This was in response to a request from the Jewish residents of Jerusalem that Nehemiah, who was serving as cupbearer (a kind of chief-of-staff) to Artaxerxes, pressure the king to grant political favors to the Jews of Yehud which would allow them to withstand the local populations hindering their work. The Levant

THE PROVINCE OF YEHUD

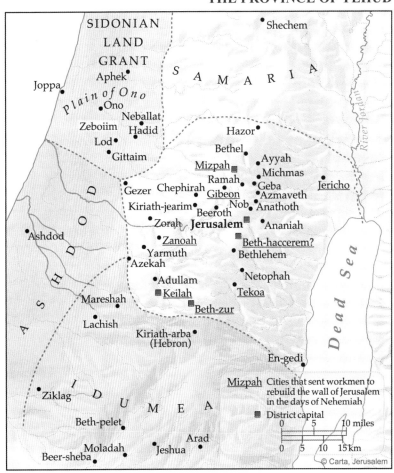

The Empire of Alexander the Great and Hellenism in the Levant

Alexander's march from west to east, across the extent of the entire known world, is widely recognized as one of the greatest turning points in history. By reversing the flow of power and goods on the grid of the ancient Near East he brought the center of influence and control forever to the West.

Alexander was the son of Philip II, king of Macedon, who claimed the ambitious goals of unifying the Greek city states of the Aegean and conquering once and for all an aging Persian Empire. Philip was assassinated in 336 B.C., and his charismatic, Aristotle-educated son, the boy with the golden mane, rode the rising tide of Hellenism all the way to the Indus Valley. Launching his campaign in 334 B.C. at the boundless age of 20, Alexander crossed the Dardanelles at Eleus, followed his legendary hero Achilles to Troy, drove through Sardis to cut the terminus of Persia's Aegean dreams, then swept across Asia Minor in just one year. His first major battle was at Issus on the Cilician Plain in 333 B.C., and Darius III (335–331 B.C.) fled for his life.

Rather than chase the ill-fated Persian monarch through Mesopotamia, Alexander headed south through the Levant in order to neutralize the Phoenician fleets that remained loyal to Persia (he could afford no behind-the-lines sweep into the Aegean). The island city of Tyre, home to the strength of the Phoenician fleet, fell in 332 B.C. after a seven-month siege during which Alexander's men built a causeway from shore (Tyre remains attached to the mainland to this day). Alexander's general Parmenio had meanwhile marched on Damascus, prompting delegations from various cities in Syria

and Palestine to approach Alexander with gestures of peace. The Macedonian army then easily subdued the rest of the city-states along the Levantine shore (Acco, Ashdod/Azotus and Ashkelon/Ascalon), with only Gaza, bolstered by Nabatean and Arab support, offering resistance. Gaza was the main Mediterranean terminus for the lucrative Arabian spice routes, and after a two-month siege the city and its economic orbit fell into Alexander's hands.

Never one to miss an opportunity, Alexander wintered in Egypt where he was welcomed as a liberator from things Persian and recognized by the oracle as the son of Amun-Ra, the true Pharaoh of Egypt. Alexander responded by founding Alexandria at the outlet of the westernmost branch of the Nile. The city was destined to become the capital of Ptolemaic Egypt, a major economic and cultural hub of the eastern Mediterranean and a leading center of the Jewish Diaspora. Leaving his general Ptolemy to run Egyptian affairs, Alexander headed northeast in the spring of 331 B.C., via the great trunk route to Damascus, then across the Euphrates and Tigris where he again caught up to Darius. The Persian army was scattered at Gaugamela later that year, and Alexander encountered no real resistance as he swept his way to the Indus Valley and steppes of central Asia.

His army refused to go any farther, and Alexander settled down to enjoy life in the East, heir to the treasure vaults of the wealthy centers of the now-beaten Persian Empire. Far removed from the simpler ways of the more democratic Macedonian court, the young emperor adopted Persian pomp, circumstance and dress, and mar-

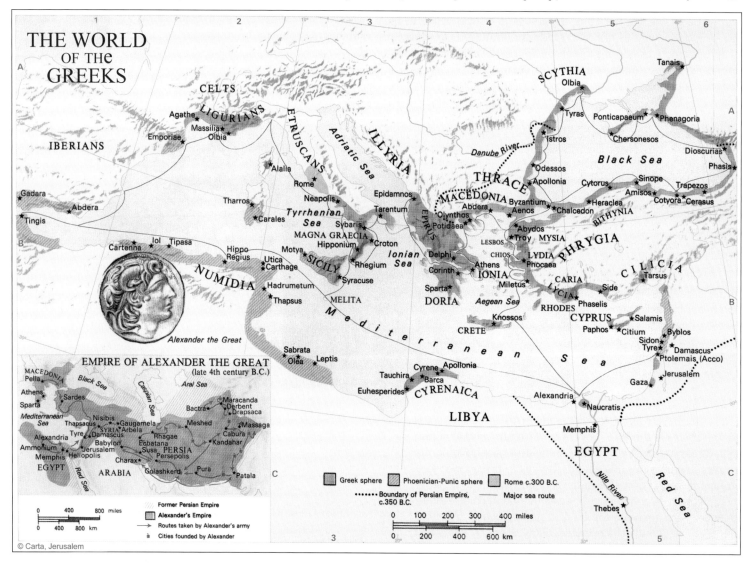

THE WORLD OF THE GREEKS

Alexander the Great

EMPIRE OF ALEXANDER THE GREAT
(late 4th century B.C.)

Greek sphere   Phoenician-Punic sphere   Rome c.300 B.C.
••••• Boundary of Persian Empire, c.350 B.C.   —— Major sea route

Former Persian Empire
Alexander's Empire
→ Routes taken by Alexander's army
⚑ Cities founded by Alexander

© Carta, Jerusalem

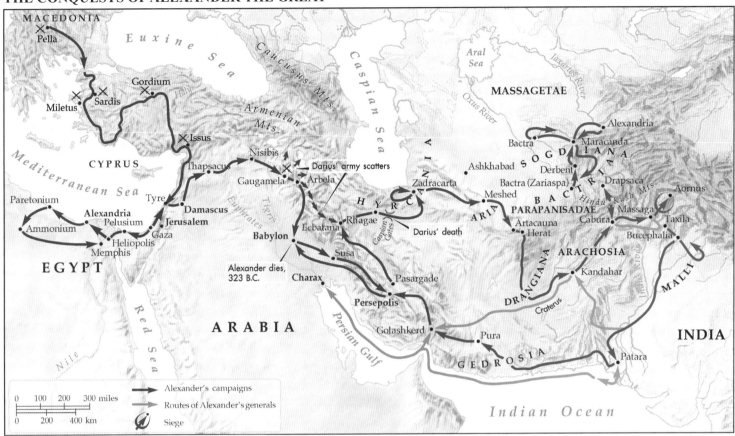

© Carta, Jerusalem

ried a Persian noblewoman in Susa amid great splendor. Alexander seems to have chosen the hoary capital of Babylon as the administrative center of his conquests. But before he could put the proper pieces in place (including designating an heir), the Macedonian king died at the age of 32 in 323 B.C., a victim of his own high living. Soldiers of similar mind settled down in his wake, sowing seeds of a new world order that merged West with East.

Alexander's kingdom fell to his generals (the Diadochi). Perhaps the most able was Antigonus Monophthalmus ("the One-eyed"), who fought for the right to be Alexander's sole heir. Other generals, such as Ptolemy of Egypt and Seleucus (who governed Babylon), already had a good thing going and could each live with a divided empire. Over the next two decades Antigonus tried three times to take Egypt, while his son Demetrius twice almost seized the strongbox of Petra. The southern Levant saw the brunt of this fighting. Antigonus was finally defeated at Ipsus in Phrygia in 301 B.C. by the combined forces of Ptolemy, Seleucus and Lysimachus, another of Alexander's generals who inherited Thrace and Asia Minor. Tcherikover has given this summary of the victors:

> They were not the greatest men of the epoch, but they were wary statesmen who knew how to pick their moment and to be content with part instead of aiming at the whole.[52]

Seleucus ended up with the largest territory, from Damascus and western Anatolia to the Indus River (this became the Seleucid Empire). Most of Seleucus' successors were named Seleucus or Antiochus, and many Hellenistic cities (polis; pl. poleis) named Seleucia and Antioch sprang up here and there. His capital was not Babylon but Antioch on the Orontes (cf. Acts 11:25–26), an administrative move that signaled the new preference for things of the west.

But like lands under the control of the Persian Empire which it replaced, Seleucus' territory lacked homogeneity or a center, and needed something around which to forge a new kind of unity. This was found in the poleis, cities established to disseminate Hellenism as the cultural flag around which to rally, and by which to foster loyalty to the king. The Seleucid kings build dozens, most in the vicinity of some ancient city that was already the center of an old political and cultural life, and with an established economic base. The chief possession of the polis was not its buildings constructed in the newest styles from Greece, but its men, especially those who held political and legal rights as citizens of the polis. Indeed, the first concern of the king in founding a polis was the formation of a citizen body, with a world view steeped in the values of Hellenism. Among these values were an emphasis placed on autonomy and liberty (in the spirit of the Greek dêmos), which freed the body politic from local encumbrances and made them subject only to their own collective propriety under the will of the king. The poleis were populated with Macedonian army veterans whose careers had ended while they were out in the field and Greek mercenaries, as well as local inhabitants who were able to receive the rights to join the citizen body. The mass of locals, however, had no citizenship rights and so did not share in the political and economic advantages of the polis. This led to sharp divisions between those who benefited from Hellenism and those who simply put up with it. In every case, the polis became a vibrant, new heir of the older, oriental town, although in practice cultural influences flowed both ways.

Down in Egypt, Ptolemy kept the southern Levant up to the springs of Panias as Egypt's historic buffer in Asia, even though his agreement with Seleucus prior to the battle of Ipsus was that everything to the border of Sinai would be included in the Seleucid Empire. The land of ancient Israel, then, again became integrated into the political and economic network of Egypt, harkening back to the days of the Ramesside Dynasty of Egypt's New Kingdom. The Ptolemies (as every king of the dynasty would be named) engaged in a lively trade with Palestine for olive oil, timber, wine and slaves. The broad fields of Galilee, forested mountains of southern Lebanon and royal estates in the Jezreel Valley were particularly im-

The Mediterranean coast north of Mount Carmel (the rise in the distance) was a prime shoreline for the penetration of Hellenism into the land of ancient Israel.

THE GREEK CITIES IN PALESTINE

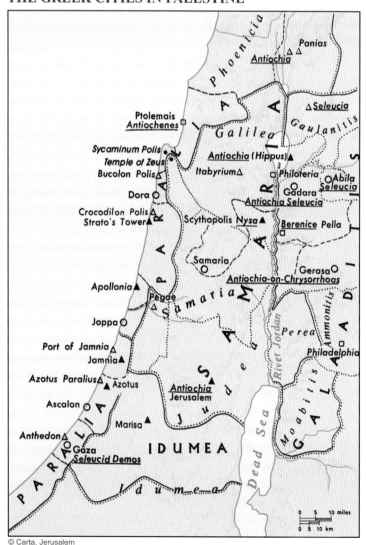

	Border of Seleucid eparchy
-----	Border of Ptolemaic city
....	Border of Ptolemaic hyparchy
PARALIA	Seleucid eparchy
Judea	Ptolemaic hyparchy
<u>Seleucia</u>	City given Seleucid dynastic name
□	City given Ptolemaic dynastic name
O	City with municipal rights under Ptolemaic rule
△	Town given Greek name
▲	City given Greek name

© Carta, Jerusalem

portant in this effort. The port of Acco, renamed Ptolemais (the only south Levantine coastal city given a Greek name), became the port of choice for Egypt's economic hold on Palestine. Details can be seen in the archive of Zenon, an Egyptian agent who arranged trade contracts during a circuit of Judea, Idumea, Transjordan and Galilee in 259–258 B.C.[53] Tyre and Sidon also remained loyal to Ptolemaic Egypt and helped the Ptolemies become the foremost naval power in the eastern Mediterranean in the third century B.C.

Within the old, unified bureaucratic political machine of ancient Egypt there was no room for Greek cities and their dangerous demands for liberty and autonomy, nor was the population of Egypt so naturally divided that a unifying force imposed from the outside was either desired or necessary. Indeed, the whole of Egypt had always been regarded as the Pharaoh's private property (the strength of the temple economies notwithstanding), and individual *poleis* would interfere with the established flow of labor and taxes upward. So only one *polis* was founded in Egypt, Ptolemais below Thebes (Alexandria was not given the status), although many old population centers inherited new Greek names.

* * * * *

Due to a lack of specific and credible contemporary sources, our understanding of the initial Jewish response to Alexander's conquest and the waves of Hellenism that rolled ashore in its wake must be left to the realm of supposition. Indeed, the Greek noun *Hellēnismos* isn't even used in the Classical Period. Jewish sources that describe events rising from the interaction of Jews with Hellenism, such as the books of Maccabees or the works of Josephus, or sources that offer reflective or exhortative commentary such as the books of the Apocrypha and Pseudepigrapha, are all later, though through them the earlier stages of the penetration of Hellenism into the Jewish Levant can be presupposed. For instance, Josephus' story of Alexander's trip to Jerusalem following the siege of Gaza, where the conquering hero was met with great hospitality and splendor by Jaddus the high priest and responded by showing obeisance to the Jews (*Ant.* xi.325–339), is certainly legendary. Yet logic suggests that Jewish leaders must have had some interaction with Alexander or his subordinates, since the Jewish pattern of relations

Remains of the Artemis (Diana) temple at Jerash (Gerasa) in Jordan, a city founded in the wake of the conquest of Alexander, still renews the call of Hellenism on the peoples of the Levant.

world conquered by Alexander, many felt as though they had little choice.

One's gateway to things Hellenistic passed through the local *polis* and its gymnasium. The latter was a military school, a school of physical fitness (where emphasis was placed on the physical body and human images), a school of civic preparation and a school of piety toward the gods. In the *polis*, those with full citizen rights took part in the general assembly of the civic body, decided city affairs, and participated in the cult of the local deity (to not do so was an insult to the dignity of the city and a political offense). One's presence at civic and religious functions was an honor, and a duty. So there was enormous incentive for the higher echelons of the native populations of the empire of Alexander and his successors, including Jews of the southern

with the Persian government was on the whole favorable and likely carried over.

In short, we can assume that a general trend toward Hellenism took hold in the southern Levant in the century following Alexander's march, primarily along the coast and through the Jezreel corridor to Transjordan. Certainly Alexander saw to it that both Tyre and Gaza were rebuilt and repopulated according to Greek ideals, and new cities such as Gerasa, Gadara, Abila and Dium, which were destined to become part of the Decapolis some centuries later, were quickly established south and east of the Sea of Galilee. The old Israelite capital city Samaria also came under Greek control, though whether by Alexander directly or his general Perdiccas is not clear. In any case Samaria was repopulated with Macedonian veterans and became the earliest wedge of official Hellenistic penetration into the hills north of Jerualem. The rise of Hellenism can also be seen through place names. Greek names were given to many old Semitic centers, even if the place was not immediately given the status of a *polis*: Beth-shean became Scythopolis; Susita was renamed Hippus, the old Ammonite capital Rabbah took the name Philadelphia; Pehel (Pella) became Berenice; Acco, as we have seen, was given the name Ptolemais. Other place names simply took Greek forms: for instance Azotus (Ashdod), Ascalon (Ashkelon), Marisa (Mareshah), Judea (Judah), Idumea (Edom) and the like. We can assume the same for personal names, at least among those who were most attracted to the benefits of Hellenism.

Hellenism, from the verb *hellēnizein*, "to speak Greek," also carries the sense of "to imitate the Greeks" or in effect "to become Greek." It reflects an all-encompassing way of life, with distinctive political, social, economic, cultural and religious aspects. Hellenistic culture was sophisticated and cosmopolitan, one that "looked good" to many outsiders, and was also inherently polytheistic, since it was tolerant of all local deities as long as their devotees wanted to participate in its full aspects. Moreover, to be a good citizen of the world and participate in the socioeconomic opportunities of the time, one had to be a good Hellenist. This was of course cultural imperialism, but given that those speaking Greek gained firm control of most of the political and economic activities of the

Levant, to want to speak Greek—and otherwise become Hellenized in at least in some of its aspects. And all this could be had through education (in the gymnasium) rather than through ancestry. There was, then, a ready-made mechanism for extensive participation in things Hellenistic for non-Greeks, especially by those who were otherwise upwardly mobile or who, for a variety of reasons, were dissatisfied with their culture of birth. Many of the wealthier local elements of a city or region took advantage of the new economic and cultural opportunities now available to them. Those toward the bottom of the socioeconomic spectrum (and this was the majority) either looked in from the outside or chose to reinforce their own ancestral traditions instead.

In the face of all of this, what were the Jews of the southern Levant to do? This was a different kind of invasion of their homeland, and at least they knew who there enemies were before! One can only assume that Jews who were willing and able to participate in the opportunities of Hellenism generally separated themselves from its religious aspects. Defining boundaries in other parts of life was more problematic. Early on, Hecataeus of Abdera, a contemporary of Alexander the Great, declared that in the Diaspora the Jews were "somewhat anti-social and hostile to strangers."[54] But over time, as the tendency toward things Hellenistic even on Israel's coastal plain grew stronger, interactions became more natural. To accommodate, the Bible—containing the very the words of God—was put into Greek (the Septuagint) in Alexandria in the third century B.C. But the closer one came to Jerusalem, and certainly among the small villages that dotted the hill country of Judea and Galilee, the more stringent were the provisions of Torah that set the tone. As an example, the writer of Ecclesiasticus (the Wisdom of Jesus ben Sirach), who lived in Jerusalem, made a cultural counter-thrust when he asserted that the only race that was truly human was the one composed of those who kept the commandments of the Lord (Eccles. 10:19; 50:27). This was a position that would lead to confrontation in the second and first centuries B.C., when the forces of Hellenism under Seleucid and Roman political control took on a tone significantly less tolerant of Judea than the Hellenism of Alexander and his early successors.

The Ptolemaic and Seleucid Empires and the Hasmonean Kingdom

Following the division of Alexander's kingdom among his generals—and the bloody jockeying for position that worked out the borders between them—the Levant south of Damascus and Tyre and the Phoenician coast up to Byblos slowly settled into Egypt's Ptolemaic Empire. Internationally Egypt was at its best when it controlled the entrance into Asia as a buffer, this time against potential aggression by the Seleucids, but when it could also commandeer the maritime economic activity of the Phoenician ports. That Ptolemaic Egypt benefited from the agricultural resources of the southern Levant (its wine and olive oil) was a plus. The Ptolemaic kings (they numbered I through XII and, with Cleopatra, covered the years 305–30 B.C.) were not particularly interested in driving the overall Hellenization process of the southern Levant (or in Egypt itself for that matter), but seemed content to let the cultural mantle spread as it may. With Egypt historically tending toward unification anyway, the need to force fraternity through the *polis* was not imminent as long as tax revenues were not impeded. At the same time, the upper echelons of native Egypt seemed to accept the Greek administrative overlay, correctly seeing it as the new way of the world. We can only assume that many of the people of the southern Levant, especially those who lived in cities along the coast and in the large inland valleys, felt the same.

Egypt was already a center of Jewish life in the Diaspora, and we can find growing, lively and productive Jewish communities concentrated in the capital city Alexandria (where the Hebrew Bible was translated into Greek), the Fayoum, and Thebes and Elephantine in Upper Egypt. The data suggests that institutions that would develop into synagogues (the word itself is Greek for "to congregate") appeared in Egypt as early as the third century B.C., though each was initially called a *proseuche*, "house of prayer." Temples to the LORD were built in Elephantine and in the eastern Delta at Leontopolis (Tell el-Yehudiyeh).

The Seleucid Empire settled into the northern Levant and the parts of Asia eastward that had been conquered by Alexander. Jewish communities thrived here as well, with Torah-observant communities in Babylon and in scattered centers in north Syria and Anatolia. This was in spite of the tendency of the Seleucid kings to plant *poleis* that would formally and intentionally disseminate Hellenism throughout their kingdom. But the Seleucid kings never forgot that on geographical criteria the entire Levant should more naturally fall to them, and began a push that would eventually win their prize.

Their means was what became known as the Five Syrian Wars, which lasted from the middle of the third to the beginning of the second century B.C. The Ptolemies were successful in holding the line during the first two wars (274–271 B.C.; 260–253 B.C.), and even made it all the way to Babylon before being pushed back in the third (246–240 B.C.). The Fourth Syrian War (221–217 B.C.) finally saw the Seleucid Empire on the rise, under the competent hands of Antiochus III (223–187 B.C.). Antiochus was able to seize the ports of Phoenicia, move into Galilee and the Jezreel Valley and push all the way to Gaza, Egypt's doorway to Asia, before he was defeated at Raphia and had to retreat back to Damascus. But the precedent had been set, and in the Fifth Syrian War (201–195 B.C.) Antiochus defeated the Ptolemaic army decisively at Panias (198 B.C.), driving Ptolemy V Epiphanes out of the Levant altogether and sealing Egypt in the Sinai. Antiochus III also campaigned successfully in Asia Minor, but within a decade would lose his holdings there to Rome, an ominous sign of things to come.

Seleucid policy sought to actively promote Hellenism in the southern Levant. It was their kings who changed the names of many oriental cities to Greek ones, though with the rise of the Hasmonean kingdom the new names didn't stick: Jerusalem became Antiochia; Gerasa was renamed Antiochia on Chrysorrhoas; Gadara became Antiochia Seleucia; and the port of Ptolemais, naturally, was renamed Antiochenes. Administratively the Seleucid kings governed Judea and Galilee from the *polis* of Samaria.

Antiochus IV took the Seleucid throne in 175 B.C. with unbounded energy to unify and hence strengthen his far-flung empire against a rising Rome by running up even higher the cultural flag of Hellenism. This had aspects of an incipient emperor cult, and Antiochus IV Epiphanes ("the Illustrious One") took steps to integrate all gods under the supremacy of the head of the Greek pantheon, Zeus. To start the process in Jerusalem the Seleucid king appointed high priests sympathetic to his goals, with Jason (an ardent Hellenizer who established a gymnasium in Jerusalem) and then Menelaus "purchasing" rights to the office through favorable bribes.

With political ends in view, Antiochus, like the kings of the Persian, Babylonian and Assyrian empires that preceded him, had to ensure a compliant population in Judea in order to launch campaigns

THE CAMPAIGNS OF ANTIOCHUS IV EPIPHANES IN EGYPT AND JUDEA

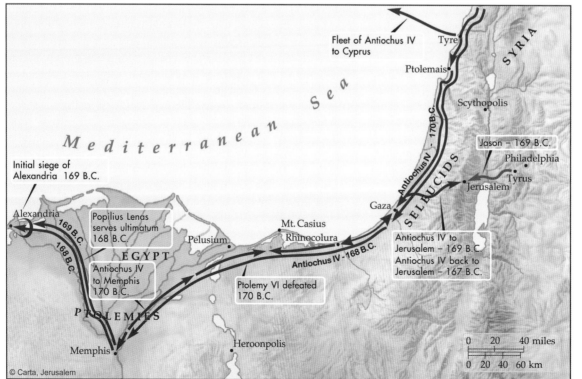

© Carta, Jerusalem

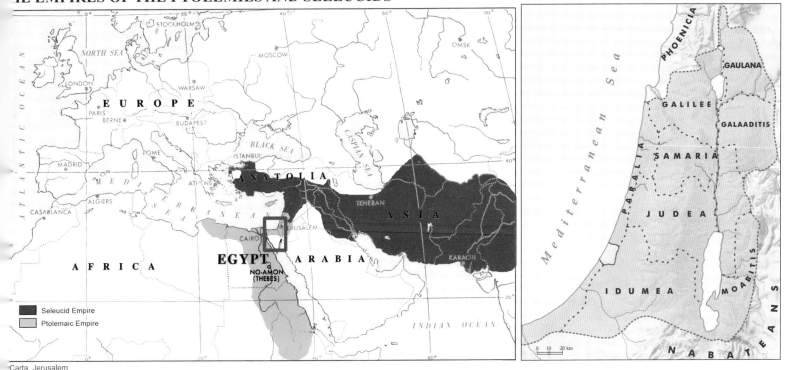

Carta, Jerusalem

into Egypt. So with the southern Levant supposedly in his pocket, Antiochus twice moved against Egypt. His first invasion was in 169 B.C., but was broken off when Jason, who had been out-bribed for the Jerusalem high priesthood by Menelaus, tried to retake the position. Following his personal money trail, Antiochus launched a bloody campaign against Jerusalem to secure Menelaus in office. His second invasion of Egypt took place the following year, but this time Rome stepped in and stopped the fight just as Antiochus reached Alexandria (Rome didn't want a unified eastern front).

Humiliated on the world stage and needing to claim at least one prize for his efforts, Antiochus took out his frustration on the people of Jerusalem. He commanded that the Jews worship Zeus and banned the exercise of religious practices essential to Judaism (keeping Shabbat and the yearly feasts, offering sacrifices and circumcision). In December 167 B.C. Antiochus turned the Temple into a sanctuary of Zeus and offered sacrifices unclean to Jewish law (1 Macc 1:41–46). Thinking he had secured the southern end of his kingdom through intimidation, Antiochus turned his attention to the Parthians on his eastern frontier, where he died suddenly of disease in 164 B.C.

While some Jews acceded to Antiochus' decrees (1 Macc 1:43), most of course did not. Opposition fused under the leadership of the family of Judas Maccabeus ("the Hammerer"), then quickly led to open revolt. The Seleucid army tried to push to Jerusalem, once from the north (1 Macc 3:1–12), twice from the west (via the Beth-horon ascent and Emmaus/Imwas; 1 Macc 3:12–4:25) and then from the south (at Beth-zur; 1 Macc 4:26–35), but were routed by Judas and his hill country warriors at every turn. Emboldened by his victories, Judas marched on Jerusalem, seized the city (except for the Akra fortress which remained in Seleucid hands) and cleansed the Temple in December 164 B.C. The Seleucid forces were not so easily defeated, however, and battles for control of the Jewish soul in its historic homeland continued for another eighteen years (1 Macc 5:1–13:33). In 142 B.C. the Seleucid king Demetrius II finally recognized Judea as an independent state in return for the support of Simon, brother of Judas Maccabeus (Judas had long fallen in battle) to his right to the Seleucid throne (1 Macc 12:33–42). The emergent Hasmonean kingdom was vastly smaller than the Seleucid

Empire in territory, population and resources. From the point of view of Demetrius, its right to exist must be seen in the *realpolitik* of the times: facing a rising Rome, a weakened Seleucid Empire needed as many friendly neighbors (cf. 1 Macc 14:39) as it could get.

*   *   *   *   *

Of course the Jews of Jerusalem and Judea saw the causes of their new-found political independence quite differently. Following the Battle of Panias they initially had welcomed the political control of Antiochus III who, reminiscent of the Persian kings, granted rights and privileges that allowed the Jews relatively free expression of their religious practices. The tendencies toward things Hellenistic were gaining steam, but at a pace that could be tolerated by most.

Everything changed with the decree of Antiochus IV Epiphanes. The Jewish revolt was prompted by Mattathias, a priest of the Hasmonean family. Mattathias lived in Modiin, a village nearly out on the Hellenized coastal plain where the world-view fight for one's soul was waged "in your face." Mattathias' son Judas took up the military side of the cause, leading the struggle in the Judean hills that resulted in the initial defeat of the Seleucid forces and cleansing of the Temple. The festival of Hanukkah ("Dedication") is celebrated to this day in celebration of Judas' achievements (1 Macc 4:36–61; Jn 10:22–23).

Upon the death of Antiochus IV (which happened the same year), Judas launched a series of defensive campaigns aimed at strengthening the Jews in their historic homeland. He fell in battle against the powerful Seleucid general Bacchides in 161 B.C.; Bacchides followed up by establishing a series of fortresses throughout Judea to squelch any further attempt at revolt. At this moment of crisis Judas' brother Jonathan assumed control of the Jewish forces and was able to gain victories and territorial concessions from the Seleucids in Samaria, Galilee, Transjordan and on the coast. His battles were territorial—for the historic "Dan to Beer-sheba" borders—but with clear implications for establishing a Jewish state. Jonathan, too, fell in the struggle (at Ptolemais; 1 Macc 12:46–48), but a third brother, Simon, survived to make peace with the Seleucid king in 142 B.C. His grateful nation conferred on Simon the title "leader and high priest forever, until a trustworthy prophet should

Coin of Alexander Janneus.

arise" (1 Macc 14:25–49).

With an independent state in hand, Simon's son and successor, John Hyrcanus (143–104 B.C.) turned the struggle from defense and protection to offense and expansion. With the tacit approval of Rome (who needed to keep the Seleucid wings clipped) Hyrcanus conquered the area of Medeba in Transjordan, Samaria (destroying the Samaritan temple on Mount Gerizim in the process) and Idumea, where the native inhabitants were compelled to be circumcised and convert to Judaism (the father or grandfather of Herod the Great was among them; *Ant.* xiii.254–258). Toward the end of his reign Hyrcanus sided with the Sadducees over against the Pharisees in internal affairs, signaling a shift toward things Hellenistic within the ruling administration of Judah. He also gave his sons (and successors) Greek names: Aristobulus and Alexander(!) Janneus. The Jewish Hasmonean kingdom was fast becoming another semi-Hellenistic despotic oriental state. But at least it was *theirs*.

The Hasmonean king Aristobulus (104–103 B.C.), called Philhellene, "a lover of the Greeks" by Josephus, conquered the Itureans in northeastern Galilee and, like the Idumeans, forced them to become circumcised (*Ant.* xiii.318). His brother and successor, Alexander Janneus (103–76 B.C.) pushed the political borders of the Hasmonean kingdom to their greatest extent. Janneus conquered all of the Greek cities on the coast south of Mount Carmel except Ascalon, completed the conquest of Galilee and Transjordan (Bashan, Gilead and Moab), and fought the Nabateans over control of the lucrative Arabian trade routes (*Ant.* xiii.323–397). It was probably also he who began to construct a series of elegant palaces and fortresses along the eastern desert frontier that would later gain fame under Herod the Great; these were the Alexandrium (Sartaba), Hyrcania, Machaerus, Jericho and likely also Masada. From the top down, the Hasmonean Kingdom was certainly starting to look Greek. In internal affairs, however, Janneus was less than successful. His favor for things Greek, combined with gross personal moral failures, brought him into open conflict with the socially and religiously conservative Pharisees. Janneus suppressed them cruelly (at one time crucifying 800; *Ant.* xviii.379–383) but made peace in the end, seeing in the Pharisees a stronger political power base for the upcoming battle against Rome than were the Jerusalem-oriented Sadducees (*Ant.* xviii.400–404).

Alexander Janneus was succeeded by his widow, Salome Alexandra (76–67 B.C.), who managed a largely peaceful reign. Yet civil war erupted when her two sons vied for control after her death. Hyrcanus II, whom Alexandra had made high priest, was favored by the Pharisees, while Aristobulus II, his younger brother and head of the army, was preferred by the Sadducees. Each asked Rome, whose own empire was quickly swallowing the Levant, for help; in 63 B.C. Pompey heartily obliged and took the kingdom away from both (*Ant.* xiv.29–79).

The rise and fall of the Hasmonean kingdom brought the issue of what was an acceptable Jewish response to Hellenism out into the open. Where was one to draw the line? Worshipping pagan gods in Judean territory became a clear "no." But what was the "yes"? Was Greek an acceptable language? If so, for what purposes? Could one become a member of the civic body of the *polis*? Or enroll in a gymnasium to receive the kind of education one needed to interact successfully with the world? Was political independence necessary to ensure the protections necessary to practice Judaism? And to what extent was Torah-oriented Judaism still relevant in the modern age?

These questions received a variety of answers (they still do), and the centuries closing the first millennium B.C. saw a rise in Jewish religious-national literature, much of it apocalyptic, advocating a return to the more straightforward days of the biblical prophets and anointed ones (e.g. the books of Esdras, Tobit, Judith, Enoch and Jubilees). The time was also ripe for the growth of religious and philosophical schools of thought representing various positions on the continuum between confrontation and accommodation. The Pharisees, for instance, represented religiously and socially conservative elements in Jewish society and found a fertile base of support among the general populace of Judea and Galilee. The Sadducees reflected the aristocratic, urban, Temple-based power circles of Jerusalem and provide examples of how to remain Torah-observant while participating in various opportunities that Hellenism had to offer. The Essenes (likely the sect of the Dead Sea Scrolls community) offered the choice of withdrawing from normative Jerusalem-based Temple practices in favor of a super-scrupulous community at an alternate site on the shore of the Dead Sea. And the Zealots, whose reason for being became sharpened after the conquest of the Hasmonean kingdom by Pompey, advocated a return to political independence, by force if necessary. In all, these were challenging times, about to be made more so as the reality of Hellenism, now firmly rooted in Judean soil, was to be joined by the heavy political footprint of Rome.

THE HASMONEAN STATE, 143–63 B.C.

The Roman Empire and the Kingdoms of the Herods

The city of Rome was founded in a melding of history and legend in 753 B.C.,[55] at about the same time that the Assyrians fixed their eyes on the southern Levant, and its inexorable rise to empire coincided with the succession of empires that invaded Judah in the centuries that followed. Archaic (or, pre-Republican) Rome was a prominent city-state of Latin and Etruscan peoples, with the Etruscans dominating city politics and spurring the forces of urbanization in the sixth century B.C. In 509 B.C. the Latins revolted and formed the Roman Republic, which lasted until Octavian (Augustus) was confirmed as emperor and "first citizen" by the Senate in 27 B.C. The Roman Republic, headed by an oligarchy of patricians, grew slowly at first, and by only the mid-third century B.C. was able to control the Italian boot, some parts directly and others through a series of alliances.

Then, in a fit of energy, Rome burst onto the world scene. Its armies first went west, where through the Punic Wars (264–241 B.C.; 218–202 B.C.; 149–146 B.C.) they secured the western Mediterranean, destroying (and eventually also rebuilding) the heavy shipping port of Carthage in 146 B.C. After the defeat of Hannibal in 202 B.C., Rome turned eastward against Macedonia and the Seleucids. The Seleucid king Antiochus III, who was poised to bring the east under his own umbrella, saw them coming. Antiochus lost western Anatolia (Pergamum) to Rome in c. 190 B.C.; the province became Asia Minor when the last king of Pergamum died in 133 B.C. Wanting to keep the east divided until it could be conquered, Rome

Pompey, as depicted on a coin.

prevented Antiochus IV from taking Ptolemaic Egypt in 168 B.C. Indeed, Rome initially acquiesced to the rights of the Hasmonean kingdom, using the efforts of the Jewish kings to keep the Seleucids and Ptolemies apart. Then they pounced.

Pompey, perhaps Rome's most powerful field general in the mid-first century, annexed Armenia in 66 B.C. He conquered Pontus, Rome's most persistent enemy in Anatolia, two years later. This gave Rome the ancient corridor linking Europe with Asia. Turning south, Pompey immediately swallowed Syria. The following year, 63 B.C., he also took Judea, a land tangled in civil war, bringing a quick and decisive end to the Jewish Hasmonean kingdom (*Ant.* xiv.1–79). Rome wouldn't close the circle of the eastern Mediterranean until the asp-induced suicide of Cleopatra VII, last of the Egyptian Ptolemaic monarchs,

THE LANDS OF THE ROMAN EMPIRE

	Under Roman control in 100 B.C.
	Under Roman control at the time of Julius Caesar's death, 44 B.C.
	Extent of direct Roman rule at the death of Augustus, A.D. 14
	Area acquired after Augustus till A.D. c.150

Oceanus Atlanticus

BRITANIA

BELGICA

LUGDUNENSIS

AQUITANIA

RAETIA NORICUM

ALPES GALLIA VENETIA

NARBONENSIS

PANNONIA

DACIA

TARRACONENSIS

ILLYRICUM (DALMATIA)

MOESIA

GALLAECIA

Rubicon

Pontus Euxinus

ARMENIA

LUCITANIA

CORSICA

ITALIA

Rome

THRACIA

BITHYNIA

GALATIA

CAPPADOCIA

COMMAGENE

PARTHIA

BAETICA

SARDINIA

MACEDONIA

Pergamum

LYCAONIA

ASIA LYCIA

CILICIA

Actium

ACHAIA

PAMPHYLIA

Mare Internum

CYPRUS

SYRIA

MAURETANIA

AFRICA PROCONSULARIS

NUMIDIA

CRETA

PHOENICIA

JUDAEA

CYRENAICA

Alexandria

Pelusium

ARABIA PETRAEA

EGYPT

0   200 mi.

0   260 km

Coin of Herod the Great.

in 30 B.C. But by then they had already planted a heavy footprint in the lands of the once-glorious ancient Near East.

One might ask what this far-off rock and sand-covered corner of the Mediterranean Sea had to offer the already over-fed appetite of Rome. The Senate and generals of the late Roman Republic have been accused of being gripped by an unsatisfied aggression that drove twin vehicles: an innate need for new triumphs on the battlefield, and a practical need for new economies to exploit. With powerful generals and loyal armies, their war machine was too large and institutionalized to stop. Be that as it may, the distant East was still expensive to conquer and hold, and there had to be both immediate and long-term gains to prompt Rome to try to incorporate its lands into those of the Republic.

The rounded, southeastern bend of the Mediterranean Sea was, perhaps, its most critical corner. On the one hand, the position of the small land of Judea provided a necessary buffer between Damascus and Egypt, two nations whose historic pattern of regional dominance was hardly stayed by the presence of foreign empires. But more importantly, this was the seam linking the wealth of the desert caravans to the growing economies of the Mediterranean world. In the first century B.C. these land routes were controlled by the Nabateans; the Iranian-based kingdom of the Parthians filled Mesopotamia beyond. Rome wouldn't absorb the Nabatean kingdom until A.D. 106 and was never able to conquer Parthia, but spent the first centuries B.C. and A.D. positioning themselves to try.

Little Judea and its neighboring provinces were, as usual, in the way. Pompey reorganized (he would say "liberated") lands from Anatolia to Judea, including those of the now-defunct Hasmonean kingdom, and incorporated them into the Roman Republic. The Greek cities on the Levantine coast and in Transjordan that had been controlled by the Hasmonean kings, plus Samaria, were placed under the supervision of the Roman proconsul in Damascus. Some of the Greek cities of Transjordan, with Scythopolis west of the Jordan River, were organized into a loose confederation called the Decapolis;[56] their rights were also subsumed under the political umbrella of Rome. Hellenistic culture was still on the upswing in the East, and with Pompey's political reorganization the economic power that the established Hellenistic structures had learned to produce now flowed directly to Rome (though Latin never replaced Greek as the language of economy and culture here). The two main economic corridors connecting the Mediterranean with the caravan routes of the Arabian Desert were Gaza to Nabatea (through the Negeb), and Ptolemais to the Decapolis via the Jezreel Valley. All roads, whether on land or sea, led to Rome.

*   *   *   *   *

Jews continued to be the majority in Judea, Perea and likely Galilee after the Roman conquest, and enjoyed a pretty decent resource base at home (technological advances were making the land about as productive as it would ever be until modern times). The reality of the Roman imperial presence was overwhelming, yet the idea of an independent Jewish state remained a live issue. Over the course

of the next two centuries Rome tried several different methods to govern the recalcitrant and freedom-loving province. In the end, the application of brute force over time won the political battle for Rome, though the Jewish soul survived to create a synagogue-based identity that thrived in countless cities and villages across Judea and the Diaspora.

The first method tried by Rome to control Judea was to appoint local leaders who would be loyal to their cause. This was the least expensive way of holding a region, and was consistent with prior practices elsewhere in the Republic by which Rome made declarations of friendship toward a conquered king. Hyrcanus II, eldest son of the Hasmonean royal couple Alexander Janneus and Salome Alexandra, was made high priest while an Idumean named Antipater, "a man of action and seditious" (*Ant.* xiv.8), was given administrative control. Idumea bordered both Egypt and the Nabatean kingdom, and so one skilled in its halls of power was rightly deemed advantageous to the Roman cause. Antipater's marriage to a Nabatean noblewoman, Cypros (*War* i.181), must have had diplomatic implications as well. In 47 B.C., the year after he defeated Pompey in Egypt, Julius Caesar bestowed Roman citizenship on Antipater and elevated him to the office of procurator of Judea (i.e., chief financial officer and the one responsible for taxation, Rome's main interest in the region; *Ant.* xiv.137–139). Hyrcanus II had supported Julius Caesar's struggle against Pompey, and out of gratitude Caesar granted the Jews of Judea special privileges: permission to rebuild the walls of Jerusalem, a reduction of their tax burden, exemption from the usual obligation of providing auxiliary troops for Roman campaigns, a guarantee of general assembly and Torah observance in the synagogue, and the return of Joppa and Lydda on the coast and certain agricultural villages of the Jezreel Valley (*Ant.* xiv.213–216). This was as far as Rome could go toward acknowledging the local rights and sensibilities of the Jews of Judea, and, all things considered, if the situation had persisted it may have been a reasonable substitute for the lost political independence of the Hasmonean kingdom.

But the workable relationship ended when the internal political turmoil that had embroiled Rome for decades caught up with Caesar on the Ides of March, 44 B.C. Antipater was also assassinated, one year later. This crisis in leadership coincided with the invasion of Judea by Parthia. Parthia was Rome's greatest nemesis in the

Tightly packed insula *housing of first-century Capernaum was typical of Galilee villages in the days of Herod. The later white limestone synagogue was built on foundation remains of the first-century synagogue, beyond.*

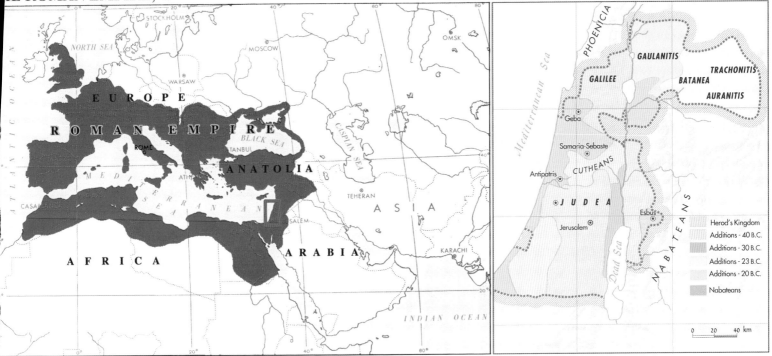

East, and their invasion was welcomed by many Jews. It was a time of general political and social turmoil, and the typical Roman response was heavy-handed: entire towns were burned and destroyed, their populations slaughtered or enslaved (*Ant.* xiv.120, 272–275; xvii.288–289, 295; *War* i.180, 219–220). The Roman Senate, at the behest of Mark Antony and Octavian, responded by appointing Herod (the Great), the ambitious eldest son of Antipater and governor of the geographically open province of Galilee, as client king of Judea (*Ant.* xiv.381–389). This was Rome's second method of attempting to control Judea, and it effectively put an end to realistic Jewish participation in the political processes of their homeland.

As for his qualifications, Herod had an Idumean father (whose family was force-converted to Judaism under Hyrcanus I) and a Nabatean mother, and these blood ties at least kept the channels for Rome's procurement of the Nabatean kingdom open. Herod's first wife, Doris, was an Idumean commoner, but his second, Mariamne (the one whom he loved to death; *Ant.* xv.218–236) was a Hasmonean princess, granddaughter of Hyrcanus II (*Ant.* xiv.300). This combination of blood and marriage made Herod Jewish enough for his Roman overlords, though hardly so for his freedom-loving subjects at home. In the eyes of the Senate Herod's main qualification was raw ambition anyway, and through it and their blessing he conquered his kingdom like any good Roman general would, by sheer force of the sword (the battles lasted from 40–37 B.C.). Herod's territory eventually included Judea, Samaria, Galilee, the coastal plain and large portions of Transjordan.

Herod's early years as client king were spent consolidating his power, a process that was complicated by the climax of internal political struggles in Rome. Cleopatra VII, with the encouragement of Mark Antony, had designs of restoring Ptolemaic Egypt's control over the southern Levant, Herod's kingdom notwithstanding. In 35 B.C. Antony gave Cleopatra large portions of the coastal plain and the Jericho oasis, taking from Herod valuable revenues related to the spice trade. But Octavian defeated Antony at the Battle of Actium in 31 B.C. and Cleopatra committed suicide shortly after, and Herod's borders became secure when he was able to convince Octavian of his personal loyalty to the new emperor (*Ant.* xv.187–201).

Armed with his victory over Antony, the Senate endowed Octavian with full imperial powers and the title Augustus ("the revered one"), thus founding the Roman Empire. Combining the ancient Near Eastern ideal of the god-king with ideas of the successors of Alexander that linked worship of the king to loyalty to the state, Augustus began a cult of the divine emperor. Although he and his successors only encouraged emperor worship (a century later Domitian demanded it), Herod nevertheless mandated that a regular sacrifice be offered on the emperor's behalf in Jerusalem. This was one of many elements of Roman political paganism that became institutionalized in Judea in the days of Herod and his successors, and forced a firm Jewish response.

To be sure, the Roman Empire was tired of war, and Augustus brought a period of *Pax Romana* and relief. This coincided with Herod's own "peace of Judea," and the so-called Jewish king spent the last two decades of his reign building physical elements of a kingdom that would wrap it with the glory and splendor of Rome. These included palace-fortresses in the desert facing the Nabateans (Herodium, Hyrcania, Masada, Cypros, Alexandrium and Machaerus, among others), urban centers such as Jerusalem (built "in the Corinthian style"; cf. *Ant.* xv.414), Antipatris, Caesarea and Samaria-Sebaste, as well as three Augusteums, temples dedicated to the divine Caesar, at Sebaste, Caesarea and Banias/Omrit. Herod's flair for megalomania impressed both Rome and his Jewish subjects, and the heavy tax burden to fund the projects was somewhat offset by the jobs it created and the overall grandeur brought to the kingdom. Like all oriental despots, Herod convinced himself that his poor subjects would somehow be content living vicariously in the shadow of his pomp.

When Herod died in 4 B.C. his kingdom was divided among three of his sons. Philip received Gaulanitis, Batanea, Auranitis and Trachonitis in northern Transjordan, an area of decidedly mixed population, and ruled until the end of his life with a reasonably fair hand (4 B.C.–A.D. 34). Antipas (called Herod the tetrarch in the New Testament; Lk 3:1; 23:7) inherited the largely Jewish and freedom-loving regions of Galilee and Perea. He managed to keep an even hand on things for most of his reign (4 B.C.–A.D. 39), but in the end was banished to Gaul by Caligula for siding with the

The remains of this temple at Omrit, just south of Banias, may well be one of the temples built by Herod the Great and dedicated to the divine Caesar, Augustus.

Parthians. Judea, Samaria and parts of the coast were given to Archelaus, and this son of Herod quickly managed to offend just about everyone in reach (cf. Mt 2:22–23). After ten long years (4 B.C.–A.D. 6), Rome, fed up with his excesses, banished Archelaus to Gaul, bringing an early end to the Herodian dynasty in Jerusalem (*Ant.* xvii.342–355).

Rome's third attempt at controlling Judea was more direct: the region was made an imperial province of mid-level equestrian rank, answerable to Caesar rather than the Senate (the Senate had appointed Herod as client king). The local governors were brought in from other parts of the empire (Pilate, for example, was from Samnium in south-central Italy). The governor of Syria, which as a high-level, imperial province stacked with legionary troops, held veto power over his colleague in Judea, and was sometimes called upon to restore order in Jerusalem. The first governors of Judea, men who were given the title *praefectus* (prefect), were reasonably sympathetic to Jewish sensibilities. Pontius Pilate (A.D. 26–36), however, exhibited all of the excesses and none of the good judgment of Herod, and like Archelaus was removed from office due to gross negligence of duty. The later governors carried the title procurator (typically the chief

THE AUGUSTEUM AT SEBASTE

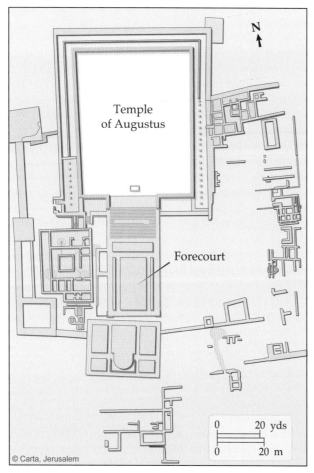

Temple
of Augustus

Forecourt

N

| 0 | 20 yds |
| 0 | 20 m |

© Carta, Jerusalem

financial officer of a province), but held full administrative power.

Fed up with the ineffectiveness of direct Roman rule, especially as it was misused by Pilate, the emperor Caligula reinstalled the Herodian dynasty by appointing Agrippa I, playboy grandson of Herod the Great, as king (A.D. 37–44). Agrippa inherited the lands of Philip and Antipas, giving him political control over an area equal to that of his grandfather. Initially welcomed by his Jewish subjects (after their experience with prefects like Pilate, a return to the Herodian line looked pretty good), Agrippa followed a well-trodden path and quickly became intoxicated with his own power. He died suddenly after a short reign (*Ant.* xix.338–352; Acts 12:20–23), and the new emperor, Claudius, reinstalled direct Roman rule.

Rome's fifth attempt at controlling Judea was, from their vantage point, the best of both worlds: a succession of procurators appointed to political control over Judea, Samaria and the coast, with Agrippa II (A.D. 50–c.100) given authority over internal Jewish religious affairs. Agrippa II was also made king of Philip's old territory in northern Transjordan, as well as scattered lands in Galilee and Perea, hopefully just enough to pacify the Jewish need for kingship. He managed a relaxed, hands-off approach to the inner-Jewish tensions that would quickly plunge his country into full-scale revolt, while taking full advantage of the personal benefits that came with his position.

The Jewish response throughout was, predictably, mixed. The institutionalization of economic opportunities led to a real separation between the powerful "haves" who could benefit from the system, and the largely disenfranchised "have-nots" on whose backs the system flourished. The latter were by far the majority, and were habitually preyed upon by not only the occupying forces of Rome but their own aristocratic ruling class. The tax burden was particularly heavy: Roman taxes were imposed on harvests, grazing rights and one's person (the poll tax); there were harbor and border taxes, and frequent though irregular duties and services demanded by soldiers at any time (cf. Mt 5:41). Obligatory temple taxes were hefty as well.

Without proper representation in the political process, the Jewish masses were left to their own devices to survive. Some found solace by focusing their identity through religious groups such as the

The inland valleys of Galilee provided fertile soil for messianic expectations in the first century A.D.—and parable language: "Some seed fell beside the road, some among the thorns, and other into good soil" (cf. Mk 4:1–9).

rugged hills of Judea, Perea and Galilee, allowed the remnant Jewish communities of the southern Levant to not only survive, but thrive. A second (and final) revolt led by Simon bar Kochba (A.D. 132–135) resulted in Rome sealing the eastern Mediterranean completely; with it the region that had been Judea was given the name Palaestina (Palestine), from Philistia, a coast-oriented view. But by now the forces of "survival Judaism" had taken firm hold.

Partly because Christians (cf. Acts 11:26) did not take part in either revolt, the Romans ceased viewing that movement as a Jewish sect and withdrew from it the official Diaspora privileges it had enjoyed while under the umbrella of Judaism. The Apostle Paul counseled his fellow believers that if they lived honest and upright lives and obeyed the Roman government, they had nothing to fear (Rom 13:1–4). By the mid-second century A.D. most Christians no longer came from Jewish origins. For better or worse, the emergent church was now weaned from its parent to come to age in a Gentile world.

Pharisees or the Essenes. Many, especially those living in Galilee, a region where comfortably-Jewish villages were wrapped up with populations that knew how to take advantage of the economic opportunities afforded by Rome, found fresh vigor looking to a Messiah figure. Galilee's fields proved to be fertile ground for divinely appointed, anointed ones who sought to bring life back around to the way it was supposed to be. Most potential messiahs placed political independence high on the list of necessary criteria, and factored revolt into the equation as well. These included Theudas, Judas the Galilean and his sons Jacob and Simeon, Athronges, the Egyptian False Prophet and the Prophet of the Desert (Acts 5:36–37; 21:38; *Ant.* xvii.278–284; xx.97–102, 168–172, 185–188). Their movements never ended happily. To them we can add the messiah "of Israel" and the messiah "of Aaron" featured in the Dead Sea Scrolls (4Q266 frag.18 iii 12). And into this matrix came Jesus of Nazareth, who spoke instead of a kingdom that would be ushered in *through* the cross (Mt 16:21, 24; Lk 13:33; 18:31–33).

Whenever Rome's local representatives were relatively benevolent (cf. Lk 7:1–5; Acts 10:1–2) and the harvests good, life could get along relatively well. But confrontation was never far away. Matters came to a head in A.D. 66 in Caesarea, Herod's shining gateway to the sea, when the Jews were expelled from the city following a clash with the Greeks. Neither the procurator Gessius Florus nor King Agrippa II could calm the situation, which quickly let to open revolt. Initial success on the battlefield prompted the rebels to proclaim an independent Jewish state. Four years of bitter fighting followed, in which Rome's legions simply smothered the valiant though overmatched forces of the Jews. Every stronghold and center that raised the flag was completely destroyed. Jerusalem bore the brunt of Rome's wrath; with it the Temple was put to the flames in the summer of A.D. 70.

Despite the threefold tragedy of the destruction of the Temple, the cessation of sacrifices and the dissolution of the high priesthood, Judaism found renewed expression through the local synagogue. A fresh emphasis on the "traditions of the fathers" in places such as Yavneh (on the thoroughly Hellenized coastal plain), Beth-shearim in the Jezreel Valley and Sepphoris, "the ornament of all Galilee" (cf. *Ant.* xviii.27) as well as in countless small villages in the more

THE KINGDOM OF AGRIPPA II

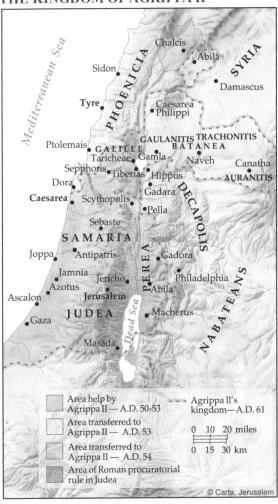

Area help by Agrippa II — A.D. 50-53	− − − Agrippa II's kingdom—A.D. 61
Area transferred to Agrippa II — A.D. 53	0 10 20 miles
Area transferred to Agrippa II — A.D. 54	0 15 30 km
Area of Roman procuratorial rule in Judea	

© Carta, Jerusalem

AFTERWORD   Such is our survey of empires and survivors in a land between. Here traffic still comes and goes, and the ones living alongside the road remain. The Pharaohs of New Kingdom Egypt sucked the resources out of Canaan, but let the people prosper as best they could in their own city-states. The Assyrians repopulated the land to sever ancestral ties. The Babylonians exiled the best and brightest, and let the rest fend for themselves. The Persians gave local concessions to foster loyalty on the edges of their frontier. The Hellenists planted their own cities in an attempt to entice the locals to a new way of life. The Romans just put their foot down for revenue and taxes. And through it all, and in spite of the terrible and seductive and productive ways of the rest of the world, God's people in Judea held to the rights of their land, to their faith-in-action, and to their relationship with God. If success is measured in what lasts, the story is still being told.

Notes and References

1   The wonderfully descriptive name "The Land Between" designating the southern Levant was coined by James M. Monson. In his *Regions on the Run* (Rockford, IL: Biblical Backgrounds, 1998), Monson provides a succinct and most helpful analysis of the role that the lands of the eastern seaboard of the Mediterranean, especially Israel, played in regard to the economic and political priorities of the empires of the ancient Near East.

2   "The Asiatic Campaigns of Thutmose III: The Annals in Karnak," in James B. Pritchard, ed., *Ancient Near Eastern Texts Relating to the Old Testament (ANET)* (Princeton: Princeton University Press, 1955), 238.

3   See the citation in note 1 above.

4   Note the list of cities conquered by Shishak that are displayed on the Bubasite Portal of the great Karnak Temple in Luxor, Egypt; Anson F. Rainey, *The Sacred Bridge* (Jerusalem: Carta, 2006), 185–189.

5   These dates follow the generally accepted Middle Chronology of Mesopotamian history; A. Leo Oppenheim, *Ancient Mesopotamia: Portrait of a Dead Civilization*, Rev. ed. by Erica Reiner (Chicago: The University of Chicago Press, 1977), 337.

6   Although we are using the word Mesopotamia in its generally accepted sense to refer to the land between the Tigris and Euphrates rivers, its original referent (note Naharaim, "two rivers") seems to have been to land lying between the Upper Euphrates and its tributary the Habor River (cp. Aram-Naharaim in Judg 3:8).

7   G. Dossin, "Les archives épistolaires du palais de Mari," *Syria* 19 (1938): 117–118.

8   F. M. Th. Boehl, "King Hammurabi of Babylon in the Setting of His Time," *Operae Minora* (Groningen: J. B. Wolters, 1953), 339.

9   "The Code of Hammurabi," *ANET*, 163–180.

10 The supremacy of Marduk was expressed in the creation epic myth Enuma Elish, in which Marduk was enthroned as the supreme god in heaven with his divine city, Babylon, the supreme city on earth; *ANET*, 60–71.

11 Hazor is mentioned 19 times in the Mari documents as a destination of economic and diplomatic emissaries, while a letter from Hazor directs the delivery of textiles, luxury goods and metals to Mari. See Abraham Malamat, "Mari and Hazor: Trade Relations in the Old Babylonian Period," pp. 45–50 in *Mari and the Bible*, Leiden: Brill, 1998; and Wayne Horowitz and Takayoshi Oshima, *Cuneiform in Canaan* (Jerusalem: Israel Exploration Society, 2006): 83–85.

12 Genesis 11:31 places Abraham's father's home in Ur of the Chaldees in southern Babylon, while the majority of the Genesis narratives place Abraham's ancestral home in and around the city of Haran, north of Mari. With this focus on northwestern Mesopotamia, it has become popular to identify Ur with Urfa (modern Sanliurfa in Turkey), a city in just north of Haran. Yet the biblical connection of Abraham's Ur with Chaldea is important in theological geography in light of Israel's eventual exile to, then return from Babylon.

13 Much work has been done to try to match the names of some or all of these kings (Gen 14:1) and/or the lands or cities that they controlled with names otherwise known from the ancient Near East. Shinar (as Babylon) and Elam are known place names; Ellasar may be Larsa. Tidal is a form of a known Hittite personal name, but Aramphel, once thought to be a form of Hammurapi, fails the equation on linguistic grounds.

14 Note the timeless assessment of Herodotus, "Egypt is an acquired country, the gift of the river [Nile]"; *The History of Herodotus*, transl. by George Rawlinson (New York: Tudor, 1928), 82.

15 Strabo, *Geography*, xvii.1.21.

16 The Horus Road was named after the protector god of the Pharaohs. An ancient map of the route can be seen on the outside of the northern wall of the hypostyle hall of the Karnak Temple. It depicts a triumphant Seti I returning across the Sinai from battle against Beth-Shean, with the Horus Road fortresses and their watering holes depicted and named. A few have been found in archaeological excavation. See "The Campaign of Seti I in Asia," *ANET*, 254; Rainey, *The Sacred Bridge*, 94–95.

17 "The Execration of Asiatic Princes," *ANET*, 328–329.

18 "Boundary Stele of Sesostris III" in Miriam Lichtheim, *Ancient Egyptian Literature*, Vol. I: The Old and Middle Kingdoms (Berkeley: University of California Press), 119.

19 Note Thutmose's own assessment: "Taking Megiddo is like taking a thousand cities!" "The Asiatic Campaigns of Thutmose III," *ANET*, 237.

20 The archive and archaeological site at Deir el-Medina, a pharonic workmen's village on the West Bank of the Nile opposite Thebes (modern Luxor) in Upper Egypt, dating to the New Kingdom, provides circumstantial though suggestive evidence of the kind of living situation that Israel might have experienced in Egypt. A. G. McDowell, *Village Life in Ancient Egypt* (Oxford: Oxford University Press, 1999).

21 "The Poetical Stela of Merneptah (Israel Stela)" in Miriam Lichtheim, *Ancient Egyptian Litera-*

ture, Vol II: The New Kingdom (Berkeley: University of California Press, 1976), 73–78.

22 Me-Nephtoah ("Waters of Nephtoah") in Josh 15:9 probably preserves the royal name Mernepthah, a place just west of Jerusalem (remains of the modern Lifta village) that was likely an Egyptian royal estate. This is the only clue in Joshua-Judges of Egypt's presence in the land, and it is opaque.

23 "The War Against the Peoples of the Sea," *ANET*, 262.

24 "The Journey of Wen-Amon to Phoenicia," *ANET*, 25–29.

25 Rainey, *The Sacred Bridge*, 186–189.

26 "The Instruction of Amen-em-opet," *ANET*, 421–425.

27 A. Leo Oppenheim, *Ancient Mesopotamia: Portrait of a Dead Civilization*, Rev. ed. by Erica Reiner (Chicago: University of Chicago Press, 1977), 95–109.

28 Note in general the Assyrian historical documents in *ANET*, 275–301, and David Ussishkin, *The Conquest of Lachish by Sennacherib* (Tel Aviv: Tel Aviv University Press, 1982), 102–109.

29 A. T. Olmstead, "The Calculated Frightfulness of Ashur-nasir-pal," *Journal of the American Oriental Society* 38 (1918): 209–263.

30 The Assyrian campaigns in the 9th through 7th centuries B.C. can be found in *ANET*, 275–301, and William W. Hallo and K. Lawson Younger, eds., *The Context of Scripture*, Vol 2 (Leiden: Brill, 2000), 261–306.

31 H. W. F. Saggs, *The Might That Was Assyria* (London: Sidgwick and Jackson, 1984).

32 This is the creative image of Assyriologist David Weisberg, Hebrew Union College, Cincinnati, OH.

33 Kurkh Stela II 90b–97, in A. K. Grayson, *Assyrian Rulers of the First Millennium B.C.*, II (858–745 B.C.), (Toronto, 1996), 23; cf. *ANET*, 279.

34 *ANET*, 280; James B. Pritchard, *The Ancient Near East in Pictures Relating to the Old Testament*, (Princeton: Princeton University Press, 1954), 351–355.

35 H. Tadmor, *The Inscriptions of Tiglath-pileser III King of Assyria* (Jerusalem: The Israel Academy of Sciences and Humanities, 1994), 62–63.

36 *ANET*, 284–285.

37 Note in particular archaeological evidence of fortifications at Lachish and Jerusalem.

38 *ANET*, 288.

39 For the official Babylonian version of events concerning Babylon during the Neo-Assyrian Period, see A. K. Grayson, *Assyrian and Babylonian Chronicles* (Locust Valley, NY: J. J. Augustin, 1975).

40 D. J. Wiseman, *Chronicles of the Chaldean Kings (626–556 B.C.)* in the British Museum (London: Trustees of the British Museum, 1956).

41 Though he is most commonly known as Nebuchadnezzar, the spelling Nebuchadrezzar which was used by Jeremiah (21:2, etc.) and Ezekiel (26:7; etc.; see the King James Version) better reflects the king's Babylonian name, *Nabû-kudurri-uṣer*. This was actually Nebuchadnezzar II, the former king of the same name reigning from 1125 to 1104 B.C. during the Second Dynasty of Isin.

42 Strabo, *Geography*, xvi.1.5.

43 This final campaign against Jerusalem is not mentioned in the Babylonian Chronicles.

44 *ANET*, 60–72.

45 H. W. F. Saggs, *The Greatness That Was Babylon* (London: Sidgwick and Jackson, 1962).

46 *ANET*, 315–316; Herodotus, *History* i.191; Xenophon, *Cyropaedia* vii.5.15.

47 Note especially inscription No. 24 from Arad in Yohanan Aharoni, *Arad Inscriptions* (Jerusalem: 46–47, 1981) and the invectives against Edom in Psalm 137:7 and Obadiah 8–10.

48 *ANET*, 315–316.

49 Herodotus, *History*, iii.89–95.

50 The phrase *eber nāri* was already used in Assyrian documents from the late eighth and early seventh centuries B.C.; R. Borger, *Die Inschriften Asarhaddons Königs von Assyrien*, AfO, Beiheft 9. (Osnabrück, 1956), 60.

51 Ran Zadok, *The Jews in Babylonia during the Chaldean and Achaemenian Periods* (Haifa: University of Haifa Press, 1979).

52 Victor Tcherikover, *Hellenistic Civilization and the Jews* (New York: Atheneum, 1979), 10.

53 C. C. Edgar, ed., *Zenon Papyri*, 4 vols. Cairo, 1925–1931.

54 Quoted by Diodorus Siculus, *Bibliotheca Historica* 40.3, 4.

55 Archaeological evidence pushes human settlement at the site that would become Rome back at least into the Neolithic Period. Archaeological remains of what is more properly called Latin Rome have been found dating to the 10th century B.C.

56 A recent suggestion argues that the name Decapolis better reflects the reality of the region only in the aftermath of the Great Jewish Revolt of A.D. 66–70; see *The Sacred Bridge*, 362.